# MARGARET ATWOOD

# Women Writers

General Editors: *Eva Figes* and *Adele King*

**Published titles:**

*Margaret Atwood*, Barbara Hill Rigney
*Charlotte Brontë*, Pauline Nestor
*Fanny Burney*, Judy Simons
*Sylvia Plath*, Susan Bassnett
*Christina Stead*, Diana Brydon

**Forthcoming:**

*Jane Austen*, Meenakshi Mukherjee
*Elizabeth Bowen*, Phyllis Lassner
*Anne Brontë*, Elizabeth Langland
*Emily Brontë*, Lyn Pykett
*Willa Cather*, Susie Thomas
*Emily Dickinson*, Joan Kirkby
*George Eliot*, Kristin Brady
*Mrs Gaskell*, Jane Spencer
*Katherine Mansfield*, Diane DeBell
*Jean Rhys*, Carol Rumens
*Stevie Smith*, Catherine A. Cirello
*Muriel Spark*, Judith Sproxton
*Eudora Welty*, Louise Westling
*Edith Wharton*, Katherine Joslin-Jeske
*Women in Romanticism: Dorothy Wordsworth, Mary Wollstonecraft
   and Mary Shelley*, Meena Alexander

**Further titles are in preparation**

Women Writers

# MARGARET ATWOOD

Barbara Hill Rigney

BARNES & NOBLE BOOKS
TOTOWA, NEW JERSEY

First published in the United States of America 1987 by
BARNES & NOBLE BOOKS
81 Adams Drive, Totowa, N.J. 07512

ISBN 0–389–20742–X (Cloth)
ISBN 0–389–20743–8 (Paper)

Printed in Hong Kong

Library of Congress Cataloging-in-Publication Data
Rigney, Barbara Hill, 1938–
   Margaret Atwood.
1. Atwood, Margaret Eleanor, 1939-    —Criticism
and interpretation.   I. Title.
PR9199.3.A8Z84    1987      818′.5409      87–1370
ISBN 0–389–20742–X
ISBN 0–389–20743–8 (pbk.)

# Contents

# Acknowledgements

I am grateful to Deans Michael Riley and John Muste and to Chairman Morris Beja, not only for the time they granted me for the completion of this book, but also for the encouragement they so generously provided. I wish also to thank Women's Studies Librarian Virginia Reynolds for her research assistance and Professors Mildred Munday and Pamela Transue for their proofreading abilities. The help of my husband, Kim Rigney, was also invaluable.

The author and publishers wish to thank the following who have kindly given permission for the use of copyright material:

Oxford University Press Canada for 22 lines from 'A Night in the Royal Ontario Museum' in *The Animals in that Country* (1968).

Margaret Atwood for 'Gothic Letter on a Hot Night' in *You are Happy* (Harper and Row, 1974).

For Julie

# Editors' Preface

The study of women's writing has been long neglected by a male critical establishment both in academic circles and beyond. As a result, many women writers have either been unfairly neglected, or have been marginalised in some way, so that their true influence and importance have been ignored. Other women writers have been accepted by male critics and academics, but on terms which seem, to many women readers of this generation, to be false or simplistic. In the past the internal conflicts involved in being a woman in a male-dominated society have been largely ignored by readers of both sexes, and this has affected our reading of women's work. The time has come for a serious reassessment of women's writing in the light of what we understand today.

This series is designed to help in that reassessment.

All the books are written by women, because we believe that men's understanding of feminist critique is only, at best, partial. And besides, men have held the floor quite long enough.

EVA FIGES
ADELE KING

# Epigraph

It is difficult to say where
precisely, or to say
how large or small I am:
the effect of water
on light is a distortion

but if you look long enough,
eventually
you will be able to see me.

MARGARET ATWOOD

# 1 Maps of the Green World

'Literature is not only a mirror', Margaret Atwood writes in *Survival: A Thematic Guide to Canadian Literature*, 'it is also a map, a geography of the mind' (18–19). In many ways, *Survival*, which Atwood describes as a 'cross between a personal statement . . . and a political manifesto' (13), is both a map and a mirror of Atwood's own poetry and fiction as well as of that tradition of Canadian art and sensibility which is Atwood's heritage. Atwood's subject in *Survival*, as it is also primary in her other literary essays, her six novels, two books of short stories, and ten volumes of poetry, is an exploration of both the creation and function of art and the assertion of its relevance in social and political contexts. For Atwood, art is a moral issue, and it is the responsibility of the writer/artist not only to describe her world, but also to criticise it, to bear witness to its failures, and, finally, to prescribe corrective measures – perhaps even to redeem.

Atwood teaches mostly through negative example: her protagonists are not very heroic heroines in the beginning of their adventures and sometimes not even at the conclusion. They are not totally reliable narrators; they may lie to the reader as they sometimes lie to themselves, or in some instances, they are even a bit mad. They are often fragmented, isolated, 'seeing poorly, translating badly' (*Surfacing*, 91). All are, in varying degrees, failed artists like those metaphorically paralysed and amputated authors whom Atwood describes in *Survival*, cut off from tradition,

1

bereft of audience and of social or political relevance. All of Atwood's writer/artist protagonists share a curious ambivalence towards their craft: they often use their fictions for the evasion of reality rather than for confrontation; they create illusion rather than transform reality. Much like Atwood's mirror images, so central to all her novels and poems, art can function, as it does for these heroines, as a way to lose the self in a vision of the self, to establish a conflict between the 'I' of the self and the 'she' of one's fiction, to become object rather than subject, to create polarities where none should exist. Like Alice in Wonderland, Atwood's heroines often move through mirrors and through their own self-deluding fictions into worlds of myth, where it is possible to lose the self and where they flounder amidst the ruins of traditional roles and obsolete images of women. But Atwood is always intent to state that, also like the mirror, art can and should function as an agent of truth, a means to knowledge and confrontation. Those of her heroines who resolve this basic conflict of illusion versus reality, who ultimately discover truth in and through art, also discover their own identities and their own humanity. In the refutation of the fantasy of the self as little-girl-lost, as innocent victim, they assert their own maturity as powerfully-creative agents – as artists.

Atwood's 'maps' for the arrival at such a destination are often complex and sometimes difficult to read. There is always more than one way to get there from here, and 'here', in Atwood's psychic geography, is sometimes the greatest enigma of all. As Atwood writes in *Survival*, 'Part of where you are is where you've been. If you aren't too sure where you are, or if you're sure but don't like it, there's a tendency, both in psychotherapy and in literature, to retrace your history to see how you got there' (112). Atwood's heroines always share with Atwood herself an ambivalence about where they have been, about their identity as Canadians, and this identity can be metaphoric as well as actual. As Atwood writes in 'Night Poem', 'In this country of water . . . your shadow is not your shadow/but your reflection' (*Two-Headed Poems*, 106). The writer heroine of *Lady Oracle* refers to herself as 'an escape artist', but she cannot escape her identity as a Canadian: '. . . my own country was embedded in my brain, like a metal plate left over from an operation' (342).

To be Canadian, for Atwood, is a state of mind, and it often has to do with psychological failure, with victimisation, with, as she writes in the Afterword to *The Journals of Susanna Moodie*, 'paranoid schizophrenia'. In all its traditional symbolism of virgin wilderness and pristine innocence, Canada is a kind of Eden of the imagination, a 'green world' which, by its very nature, is subject to invasion and oppression by its stronger southern neighbour. Canada represents victimisation of the kind that Atwood describes in *Survival* under the classification of 'basic victim positions' and, in this way, Canada is essentially 'feminine' in a powerfully 'masculine' world. Such symbolism has its parallel in Atwood's novels and poems of sexual politics: men victimise and oppress women, who in turn exert a passive-aggressive power in the protestation of their own innocence. Atwood's innocent and at least symbolically virginal heroines, she implies, must, like Canada as a whole, refute the illusion of their own innocence, recognise their complicity in the destructive cycle of power and victimisation, and thus confront their own reality, divided and schizophrenic as that reality may be. Just as Atwood's heroines must move from innocence to confrontation, so Canada as a nation must recognise and confront its own political identity.

Atwood's negative evaluations of Canada as fact and as symbol are always tempered, however, by nostalgia: it is home to which one returns for safety as well as for escape. For the desperate heroine of *The Handmaid's Tale*, for example, Canada becomes the only sane haven in an insane world, the only possible refuge from slavery, and this, in fact, has been Canada's historical tradition. It is the 'mother' country for which one longs, but which one yet rejects. There is always, in Atwood, the necessity to redefine the mother, to return to one's childhood home, to explore the past in order to confront the present. As the orphaned and isolated protagonist of *Surfacing* begins her actual journey into the Canadian backwoods of her childhood and her psychological journey toward selfhood, she says, 'I can't believe I'm on this road again . . .' (9). 'This road' is both 'map' and 'trap', both imprisoning convention and necessary tradition. So, the literary tradition of Canada inhibits Atwood as artist, yet paradoxically serves her as guide. As she writes in *Survival*, '. . . having bleak ground under your feet is better than having no ground at all. Any map is better than no map as long as it is accurate, and knowing your starting points and your frame of reference is better than being suspended in a void' (246).

Certainly, Atwood's Canadian tradition provides her with a preponderance of images and archetypes which are poetically and novelistically intrinsic to her work. Not only do her heroines share a symbolic identity with Canada in their victimisation and initial powerlessness, but they also affirm selfhood and power within the context of Canadian literary tradition. What Atwood has described in *Survival* as a prevailing fertility myth involving the archetype of 'the Great Canadian Baby', for example, becomes, with some significant transfigurations, a metaphor in her own fiction for a rebirth of the self into artist. Those of Atwood's heroines who do not bear children are correspondingly failed artists, failed adults locked into their own childhoods, doomed perpetually to the role of virginal young woman which Atwood characterises in *Survival* as the 'Diana' stereotype so prevalent in Canadian fiction.

Marian in *The Edible Woman* never truly grows up, partly because she rejects and denies her own feminine powers of procreation, which again are symbolic of her potential for artistic creativity. The heroine of *Surfacing*, on the other hand, assumes her own integration and thereby her sanity with the symbolic re-creation of her self in the conception of a baby. Also for Jeannie (Genie?) in Atwood's short story, 'Giving Birth', the baby itself is a metaphor for art and thus for creative power. The child's first word, says the narrator, will be 'something miraculous, something that has never yet been said' (*Dancing Girls*, 226). Atwood's own daughter, the subject of a number of poems including 'Spelling', receives the legacy of her mother's art, which is both how to spell and 'how to make spells'; Atwood writes in this poem, 'A child is not a poem,/a poem is not a child./There is no either/or', but she hastens to qualify with the word, 'However' (*True Stories*, 63). The child thus is both created and creative. In another poem, 'A Red Shirt', Atwood bestows upon her daughter the potential to dance and to dispel myths. The colour red loses its association with blood and thus its fatal implications as the child puts on the red shirt which again is the product of her mother's art, waves her arms, and makes the world 'explode with banners' (*Two-Headed Poems*, 105).

Within the Canadian tradition, Atwood writes in *Survival*, the 'Great Canadian Baby' too frequently becomes the 'Great Canadian Coffin', an image of 'stunted or doomed fertility' (208). So, too, in Atwood's novels and poems, the fertility myth as a metaphor for art is frequently inverted: babies are aborted, born dead or malformed, just as art is sometimes misconceived. The possible birth of a monster obsesses Lesje in *Life Before Man*; the poisoned women in *The Handmaid's Tale* are likely to give birth to 'shredders' rather than to normal children. The Frankenstein's monster image is recurrent, particularly in Atwood's poetry, the artist/woman/Frankenstein having 'given birth' to a terrible art form she cannot control. In 'Five Poems for Dolls', the hideously-smiling dolls represent aborted babies, or babies never conceived. In 'Useless', 'words we never said' are equated with 'our unborn children' (*You Are Happy*, 10). In 'Chaos Poem', the speaker 'can hear/death growing in me like a baby with no head' (*You Are Happy*, 14). In *The Journals of Susanna Moodie*, the speaker shocks us with the observation that 'unborn babies/fester like wounds in the body' (42). For the wife in Atwood's short story, 'The Resplendent Quetzal', her own dead baby is re-created in the grotesque Christ child she steals from a plaster crèche. The controlling image in *Two-Headed Poems* is that of Siamese twins, 'Joined Head to Head, and still alive' (59). In *Surfacing*, the protagonist considers that her aborted baby is her Siamese twin, the other half of her self which is also her self as artist. The woman artist, Atwood makes clear at various points in her writing, is herself a kind of Siamese twin: 'the woman who is a writer who is also a woman' is like 'Siamese twins pulling uneasily against each other, the writer feeling suffocated by the woman, the woman rendered sterile by the writer' (*Second Words*, 172). The paradox is inescapable: 'The heads speak sometimes singly, sometimes/together, sometimes alternately within a poem./Like all Siamese twins, they dream of separation' (*Two-Headed Poems*, 59).

As the fertility myth, in all its manifestations, is central to Atwood as to much of literary tradition, including Canadian literature and folk tales, so episodes of drowning, of becoming submerged, of travelling beneath water or beneath the earth dominate Canadian tradition and Atwood's work as well. As in many literatures, such images imply a rebirth, a return, a 'surfacing', a regeneration, all leitmotifs for Atwood. In *Procedures for Underground*, for example, the narrative voice is again a kind of Alice in an underground Wonderland, a mythic region of the psyche where wonders are both bizarre and beautiful yet always threatening, always containing the possibility of transformation or metamorphosis, perhaps even into the sub-human or the supra-human. Also in *Surfacing*, the protagonist dives too deeply into the lake and experiences another kind of reality that is replete with monsters and yet with truth. All Atwood's heroines experience such a sojourn in magic realms, to whatever symbolic or imagistic degree; all incarnate the mythological Persephone's part-time residence in the underworld, or Alice's adventures down in the rabbit burrow. To 'surface' from such experiences, to return to what is conceived to be 'reality', as Alice returns to a waking world and Persephone from the underworld to her mother's meadow, is to achieve a special knowledge, to assume the role of artist, which is synonymous with 'seer', to become, as in Canadian tradition, the shaman.

The role of the artist, particularly in contemporary society, is, for Atwood, shamanistic, even though she indicates throughout her work a realisation of the dangers for the artist herself that are implicit in such a distinction. There is the inherent moral obligation to use one's art to create life rather than reduce it to artifact, to avoid the misuse of art which is the curse of 'the girl with the Gorgon touch' and of the female Frankenstein, both of whom appear throughout Atwood's fiction and poetry. One of Atwood's few heroines who does not misuse her art is Circe in 'Circe/Mud Poems'. Her role, certainly, is that of shaman:

> People come from all over to consult me, bringing
> their limbs which have unaccountably fallen off,
> they don't know why, my front porch is waist deep
> in hands, bringing their blood hoarded in pickle
> jars, bringing their fears about their hearts, which
> they either can or can't hear at night. They offer me
> their pain, hoping in return for a word, a word, any
> word . . . . (*You Are Happy*, 49)

Art, then, is the magic power to cure, to comfort, to transform. Circe can transform men into pigs, but, more importantly, pigs into men, lover into human being. In a real sense, Atwood's poems and fiction also do this: they turn magic into art, myth into reality, archetype into recognisable human being. The real power of art, for Atwood, is to enhance life, to make it more fully humane and thus to obliterate the polarities between the real and the fantastic.

Myth and magic are thus not destinations on Atwood's literary map, but places through which the artist passes on her way to 'here'. 'This is how I got here', begins the heroine of *Bodily Harm*, and the poems in *Procedures for Underground* are, in one respect, a parody of a travel guide, noting the wonders and dangers of the journey but always pointing the direction home. Myth belongs then to the geography of childhood, to the psychology of a Canadian past. Atwood describes the mythologies inherent in Canadian children's literature as '. . . a world of frozen corpses, dead gophers, snow, dead children, and the ever-present feeling of menace, not from an enemy set over against you but from everything surrounding you' (*Survival*, 30). Atwood's poetic images and novelistic plots are replete with similar references, with such feelings of menace. Mistaken and misguided heroines consistently 'transform' themselves into animals, particularly small, helpless ones of the hunted variety: Marian in *The Edible Woman* is like a rabbit who must burrow to safety to avoid the evil male as hunter. The protagonist of *Surfacing* seeks safety by trying to 'grow fur', by abdicating her human status. Joan Foster in *Lady Oracle* is haunted and persecuted by a mysterious person who leaves mutilated small animals, effigies of Joan herself, at her door. Lesje of *Life Before Man* identifies with dinosaurs (not small animals certainly but nevertheless powerless to prevent their own extinction) who live in some imaginary prehistoric green world which represents yet another variation on the underground existence. Even the titles of poems, like *The Animals in That Country*, testify to Atwood's fascination with animal imagery and her recognition of the necessity to move beyond such seductive yet childish identification, an identification, finally, which contributes to a view of the self as victim.

Victimisation, according to Atwood, is the subject of a great deal of mythology, Canadian and otherwise. The victimised heroines of fairy tales are also frequently a source of identification for Atwood's protagonists, and they inevitably prove to be destructive models. In *Survival* Atwood describes the traditional heroine of Canadian fiction as a Rapunzel or as a Lady of Shalott, an image of the woman/artist imprisoned in a tower of mythology which is of her own construction. Atwood repeatedly refers also to the Little Mermaid, that archetypal victim/artist who sacrifices her tongue in order to grow legs so that she can search for the handsome prince. Atwood writes in *Second Words* about the woman as writer, the paradox that 'If you want to be female, you'll have to have your tongue removed, like the Little Mermaid' (225).

Atwood's most pervasive fairy-tale image, also related thematically to the Little Mermaid, is perhaps that of the 'dancing girl', the possessed victim in 'The Red Shoes', and of her descendent, Moira Shearer in the film of the same name. In the film, the dancer must dance herself literally to death, having made the fatal choice for art over love. In *Second Words*, Atwood talks about the impact of the myth and the film on a generation of little girls who '. . . were taken to see it as a special treat for their birthday parties. . . . The message was clear. You could not have both your artistic career and the love of a good man as well, and if you tried, you would end up committing suicide' (224). All of Atwood's heroines, including the Persephone voice of *Double Persephone*, are 'dancing girls' for at least a time, denying their identities as artists, permitting the removal of their tongues, and opting for victimisation in the games of sexual politics. In her poem, 'A Red Shirt', Atwood expresses the desire to protect her daughter from such roles: '. . . she should/keep silent and avoid/red shoes, red stockings, dancing./Dancing in red shoes will kill you' (*Two-Headed Poems*, 101). The idea of dancing one's self to death becomes, finally, a dominant irony in *The Handmaid's Tale* in which the heroine, dressed from head to toe in red, faces the possibility of dancing from a hangman's noose.

Atwood derives her mythic metaphors from diverse sources: classical accounts of metamorphoses (particularly in the 'Circe/Mud Poems'), gothic horror stories, the ghost tales of Henry James, Christian concepts of martyrdom, Canadian folklore, and fairy tales for children, which, among others, will be explored in the following chapters. But always her use of myth is a deconstructive one; she disassembles the myth to reconstruct it in terms of the modern female psyche and the special circumstances of the contemporary female *kunstlerroman*. Her protagonists are always explorers through tradition and myth in search of a new identity and in search of a voice, a tongue, a language, an art, with which to proclaim that identity.

Particularly in this sense, Atwood can be seen as a 'feminist' writer: she is concerned for the psychological and physical survival of women, and she sees this in terms, not merely of individual survival, but of sisterhood. Almost always there is a sister-figure in Atwood's fiction, a secondary character, sometimes a confidant, who often aids the protagonist, even if the protagonist solipsistically refuses to recognise her value. Women friends, being subject to the faults of the rest of humanity, may turn out to be as treacherous as men, as is the case with Ainsley in *The Edible Woman* and with Anna in *Surfacing*, but they may also serve as unconditional supporters and faithful allies in a way that men never do. Moira in *The Handmaid's Tale* and Lora in *Bodily Harm*, for example, are more heroic figures than are the heroines themselves.

Too, Atwood frequently incorporates the theme of the rediscovered mother, a pervasive concern in feminist literature as a whole from *Jane Eyre* to Adrienne Rich. In such poems as 'Five Poems for Grandmothers' (*Two-Headed Poems*), Atwood makes clear her sense of the bond among women, particularly of that bond which is of blood. In 'A Red Shirt' also, Atwood writes of '. . . the procession/of old leathery mothers . . . passing the work from hand to hand,/mother to daughter,/a long thread of red blood, not yet broken' (*Two-Headed Poems*, 102). Like Persephone, however, most of Atwood's protagonists in the novels have 'lost' their mothers, a factor which contributes to or is symptomatic of their more general homelessness and isolation. Joan Foster in *Lady Oracle* cannot recognise herself at least partly because she cannot recognise a reality for her mother. The heroine of *Surfacing* is one of the few who rediscovers her mother, and thus rediscovers herself.

Atwood's sister and mother figures, however, are human women rather than witches, goddesses or Demeter figures, and it is the protagonists' recognition of this human status which is a key to the discovery of their own identities. Even that archetypal woman as artist, the Siren, pleads for a restoration of her humanity: in 'Siren Song', she will share her secret song in order to get out 'of this bird suit . . ./I don't enjoy it here/squatting on this island/looking picturesque and mythical/with these two feathery maniacs' (*You Are Happy*, 38–39). Perhaps Atwood's desire to portray women as individuals rather than as incarnations of myth, her attempt to 'take the capital W off Woman' (*Second Words*, 227), is the aspect of her work which provides the greatest problems for some feminist critics. Atwood's view that women share in the guilt for their victimisation, that women's problems are 'part of a larger, non-exclusive picture . . . men can be just as disgusting, and statistically more so, towards other men . . .' (*Second Words*, 282), indicates that Atwood is as prescriptive towards the feminist movement as towards the rest of society. Atwood has also made clear in a number of interviews that she is against the idea of 'power' in general, whether held by men or women: 'there's no point in destroying a male child *instead* of a female one'.[1] Again, women, in Atwood's terms, are not myths but human beings capable of all the evils and faults that term implies, and such a belief does not render her less a feminist.

Atwood has grown up with the contemporary women's movement and, like most of the best writers today, she has transcended its infancy along with her own. From what Atwood herself has termed in *Second Words* the 'protofeminism' of *The Edible Woman*, her work has developed into an increasingly revolutionary vision of women's place in a profoundly political world, a vision based on women's humanity and their potential acceptance of human responsibility, for evil as well as good. Like many other feminist writers, she is concerned most specifically with the role of women as artists and with the political implications of that role. More than men, women artists are subject to role prescriptions and the necessities of the mundane; as the speaker/artist complains in 'Small Poems for the Winter Solstice', 'You think I live in a glass tower/where the phone doesn't ring/and nobody eats? But it does, they do/and leave the crumbs and greasy knives' (*True Stories*, 33). Childbirth and artistic creativity may be metaphorically linked, but in a practical world they may also represent a conflict: 'and I wonder how many women/denied themselves daughters,/closed themselves in rooms,/drew the curtains/so they could mainline words' (*True Stories*, 63).

In the first place, to be a woman artist may be a contradiction in terms; the 'red shoes' paradox and the

Siamese twins conflict are by no means obsolete. In her short story 'Lives of the Poets', Atwood depicts the poet protagonist on a lecture tour; in pursuit of her art, she loses her husband to the attentions of another woman. Her every public appearance is preceded by a nose bleed, symbolic of the price of art: 'Blood, the elemental fluid, the juice of life, by-product of birth, prelude to death. The red badge of courage' (*Dancing Girls*, 191–92). Regardless of the price, however, Atwood condemns her heroines to the choice for art. Even in her own life, as Atwood has stated, there is always a contradiction in roles:

> You would come to a fork in the road where you'd
> be forced to make a decision: 'woman' or 'writer'. I
> chose being a writer, because I was very determined,
> even though it was very painful for me then (the late
> fifties and early sixties); but I'm very glad that I
> made that decision because the other alternative
> would have been ultimately much more painful. It's
> more painful to renounce your gifts or your direction
> in life than it is to renounce an individual.[2]

Atwood's heroines have always to learn this same lesson. For Atwood, the female *kunstlerroman* is both fictive subject and political autobiography.

The literary tradition from which Atwood derives her inspiration is, to a great extent, a female tradition. Her studies, both academic and informal, began with an interest in the nineteenth-century British novel, a genre dominated by such female giants as the Brontës, Jane Austen and George Eliot. Canadian literary tradition, too, according to Atwood, is heavily populated by women authors. And, if her many book reviews, some of which are reprinted in *Second Words*, are an accurate indication, Atwood's current literary interests are also in the area of women writers, for she has written widely on the works of such contemporary

American feminist authors as Adrienne Rich, Sylvia Plath, Anne Sexton, Marge Piercy, Kate Millett, and Tillie Olsen, as well as on those of Canadian women writers such as Margaret Laurence, Marie-Claire Blais, Margaret Avison, and Audrey Thomas, all of whom have, to varying degrees, influenced Atwood's own work. In these analyses of the works of other writers (Atwood as critic will be discussed in Chapter 7), Atwood proves herself an excellent feminist critic, not only in the expansion of the canon of women writers, but in the deconstruction of male texts as well, a task which she undertakes with a great deal of characteristic dry humour in such volumes as *Murder in the Dark*. In defining a 'male' literary style as opposed to a female aesthetic, Atwood jokes, 'Last time we looked, monosyllables were male, still dominant but sinking fast, wrapped in the octopoid arms of labial polysyllables, whispering to them with arachnoid grace: *darling, darling*' (*Murder in the Dark*, 34). All of Atwood's works, no matter how ultimately and seriously profound, do not neglect the aspect of humour, and her style is *feminist* humour most often directed against the inflated egos of men, especially men who wear cloaks.

Atwood's male characters in both the poetry and fiction, are, however, most often depicted as human beings rather than as archetypes or romantic images. Only men who think of themselves as superhuman, like Ulysses in the 'Circe/Mud Poems', are ultimately ridiculous, even boring. Circe's greatest feat of magic or art is her transformation of Ulysses from god into human being: 'Men with the heads of eagles/no longer interest me/or pig-men, or those who can fly/with the aid of wax and feathers', she remarks. In fact, their fallibility is amusing: 'on hot days you can watch them/as they melt, come apart,/fall into the ocean'. Both Atwood and Circe prefer '. . . the others,/the ones left over/the ones who have escaped from these/mythologies with barely their lives;/they have real faces and hands . . .'

(*You Are Happy*, 47). Atwood ponders the fallibility of the demon lover in her short story, 'Hair Jewellery', and concludes that 'What Psyche saw with the candle was not a god with wings but a pigeon-chested youth with pimples, and that's why it took her so long to win her way back to true love. It is easier to love a daemon than a man, though less heroic' (*Dancing Girls*, 105). For Atwood, men as individuals are much like women as individuals, subject to the same polar thinking, torn between good and evil: 'I give you Albert Schweitzer in one corner, Hitler in another', she writes in *Second Words* (414).

However, the Hitler bogey becomes increasingly dangerous as Atwood's political consciousness and her feminism become more defined in the later works. Men are dangerous, she perceives, not because they are intrinsically more evil than women, but because they are in control, because they have the power. In 'Liking Men', for example, Atwood sees the benign aspect of male power, '. . . quiet and sane. Knowing what to do, doing it well. Sexy'. But she also realises that men make war; they are capable of rape and murder:

> Now you see rows of them, marching, marching;
> yours is the street-level view, because you are lying
> down. Power is the power to smash, two hold your
> legs, two your arms, the fifth shoves a pointed
> instrument into you; a bayonet, the neck of a broken
> bottle, and it's not even wartime, this is a park, with
> a children's playground, tiny red and yellow horses
> . . . who did this? Who defines *enemy*? How can you
> like men? (*Murder in the Dark*, 54)

Each novel and poem of Atwood's seems more 'feminist' than the last; her catalogue of the atrocities perpetrated on women, from chastity belts to genital mutilation and prostitution, which she describes in 'A Women's Issue', is as terrifying as the descriptions by feminist-theologian Mary Daly in *Gyn/Ecology* of identical acts of violence. Atwood's anger in 'A Woman's Issue' is unmitigated by her usual humour, although the sense of irony is always present: she writes of the tortured women of the poem, 'You'll notice that what they have in common/is between the legs. . . . Who invented the word *love*? (*True Stories*, 55).

But perhaps finally we must categorise Atwood's most recent work (if such categorisation is desirable at all) as something like 'radical humanism'. From her early disclaimers of aspiration to a political voice, her frequent statements that 'books don't save the world', she has moved steadily towards a firm commitment to human rights and the conviction that if books, in fact, don't save the world, then nothing else can either. From early essays reprinted in *Second Words* we infer that Atwood's philosophy was one of reservation, that there is '. . . a questionable value of writers, male or female, becoming directly involved in political movements of any sort: their involvement may be good for the movement, but it has yet to be demonstrated that it's good for the writer' (190). Later, however, particularly as manifested in *Bodily Harm*, *True Stories* and *The Handmaid's Tale*, that sentiment has changed, perhaps due to Atwood's discovery of Amnesty International and her growing recognition that we live in an increasingly violent and power-oriented society. The facts and political realities, atrocities committed in the name of ideology, terrorism and brutality, become crucial for Atwood, 'not because the writer is or is not consciously political but because a writer is an observer, a witness, and such observations are the air he breathes' (*Second Words*, 394). Politics, which Atwood defines in deceptively simple terms as 'who has the power', becomes a matter, not of choice, but of human responsibility for which both novel and poem become the vehicle.

Largely for this reason, I have chosen not to separate discussions of Atwood's poetry from discussions of her fiction in the following chapters. Although Atwood has stated in an interview that, as a writer of prose, she is not just a 'somewhat different' personality from the writer of poetry, but 'an almost totally different one',[3] the poems and novels are nonetheless related ideologically and even stylistically. Atwood's novels and short stories are poetic in style and diction, and her poems have a distinct narrative quality. The heroines of both poems and novels are similar in character and in psychological condition. Most important, however, is the fact that both fiction and poems are in the form of testaments: 'eye-witnesses, I-witnesses' (*Second Words*, 203). They, in essence, comprise one story, which Atwood calls 'the story of the disaster which is the world'. Atwood herself is chronicler of this disaster: '*I only am escaped alone to tell thee*: When a story, "true" or not, begins like this, we must listen' (*Second Words*, 350).

# 2 Alice and the Animals: *The Edible Woman and Early Poems*

On one level, Atwood's first published novel, *The Edible Woman*, is a 'realistic' and often comic account of a young woman's rather prosaic life in Toronto. Marian MacAlpin attends her job at 'Seymour Surveys', a marketing research firm; she lives with a roommate, Ainsley; she becomes engaged to a very proper young man, Peter; she meets a second, less proper young man, Duncan; she becomes disenchanted with the first; she stops eating; she breaks off her engagement; she begins to eat; she ends with no lover, no job, no roommate, but with a remarkably healthy appetite. Readers, however, should not be deceived by what appears to be a simple plot. Atwood's novels are never on one level; they are often, like *The Edible Woman*, quite elaborate detective stories in which the reader must become the detective, and Atwood herself, as she indicates in *Murder in the Dark*, is the criminal: '. . . that's me in the dark. I have designs on you. I'm plotting my sinister crime, my hands are reaching for your neck or perhaps, by mistake, your thigh. . . . Just remember this, when the scream at last has ended and you've turned on the lights:

by the rules of the game, I must always lie' (*Murder in the Dark*, 30). Thus Atwood invites our participation in her creations; the images and allusions are clues, and the reader is challenged to interpret the evidence, to divine the lies, to reassemble and to propose hypotheses for solutions.

Like all of Atwood's heroines, Marian lives a double life, the more interesting of which is her psychic 'underground' life, her Alice-in-Wonderland-like dream existence. Atwood's invitation to interpretation in this literary context is provided by a long passage in which 'Fish', appropriately enough an English graduate student and adept at fishing for symbolic interpretations of literature, explains his current research project to Marian and also provides a number of clues for the reader of *The Edible Woman*:

> Of course everybody knows *Alice* is a sexual-identity-crisis book that's old stuff, it's been around for a long time, I'd like to go into it a little deeper though. What we have here, if you only look at it closely, this is the little girl descending into the very suggestive rabbit-burrow, becoming as it were pre-natal, trying to find her role . . . as a Woman. Yes, well that's clear enough. These patterns emerge. Patterns emerge. One sexual role after another is presented to her but she seems unable to accept any of them, I mean she's really blocked. She rejects Maternity when the baby she's been nursing turns into a pig, nor does she respond positively to the dominating-female role of the Queen and her castration cries of 'Off with his head!'. . . . And right after that you'll recall she goes to talk with the Mock-Turtle, enclosed in his shell and his self-pity, a definitely pre-adolescent character; then there are those most suggestive scenes, most suggestive, the one where her neck becomes elongated and she is accused of being a serpent, hostile to eggs, you'll

remember, a rather destructively-phallic identity she indignantly rejects; and her negative reaction to the dictatorial Caterpillar, just six inches high, importantly perched on the all-too-female mushroom which is perfectly round but which has the power to make you either smaller or larger than normal, I find that particularly interesting . . . . (199)

Patterns do indeed emerge, in spite of Fish's inflated rhetoric and his fascination with the grotesque (yet another of his projects involves 'Womb-Symbols in Beatrix Potter'), for Marian is also in search of her identity as 'Woman', although her search is not a conscious one. Like Alice, she lives partly in a surreal world of the subconscious where the bizarre is an aspect of the logical, the physical world a manifestation of the psychological. Marian's body, like Alice's, is subject to sudden metamorphoses, transformations which are symbolic of her mental state: 'Marian gazed down at the small silvery image reflected in the bowl of the spoon: herself upside down with a huge torso narrowing to a pinhead at the handle end. She tilted the spoon and her forehead swelled, then receded' (150). At another point, she dreams that her toes and fingers are turning transparent and melting into jelly. Also like Alice, Marian symbolically burrows into rabbit holes; early in the novel she eats or drinks anything labelled as edible; she considers Ainsley's suggestion that she carry a bouquet of mushrooms at her wedding; and she insists on seeing both herself and her friends as Mock-Turtles and varieties of other quasi-human species. Quite certainly, Marian is like Alice in that she regards babies as pigs.

That 'female identity' which Marian's prefeminist society presents to young women is clearly marriage and maternity, in that order. Atwood explains that *The Edible Woman* was conceived 'while gazing . . . at a confectioner's display window full of marzipan pigs . . . I'd been speculating for some time about symbolic cannibalism. Wedding cakes with sugar brides and grooms were at that time of particular interest to me' (*Second Words*, 369). *The Edible Woman* could, in fact, be seen as a case study in aversion to female roles, much as Fish interprets *Alice in Wonderland* in the paragraph cited above. Real-life brides and grooms, in Marian's experience, do, in essence, 'eat' each other, and maternity also becomes associated with cannibalism. Every other young woman of Marian's acquaintance is either pregnant or would like to be, and Marian finds herself surrounded with fecundity of a nature she finds appalling.

The novel opens at the beginning of the Labour Day weekend, an appropriate holiday on which to visit Clara, an old college friend who is soon expecting her third child, an entity as unwelcomed as the first two. The formerly-beautiful Clara has, as Marian perceives her, been metamorphosed into the very serpent which Alice is accused of becoming in Fish's explanation: she looks to Marian like a 'boa-constrictor that has swallowed a watermelon' (30). Her pregnancy is a kind of mental 'vegetation', symbolised by the stylised flowers, more ominous than decorative, on her maternity smock which 'moved with her breathing, as though they were coming alive' (36). Children hang from her body like leeches; they scream and wet on the guests' clothing; they have bowel movements in inappropriate places; and, in general, behave in an extremely piggish fashion. They are, after all, products of what both Marian and Clara perceive as a kind of disease; as Clara characterises her pregnancy: 'Maybe it isn't a baby at all but a kind of parasitic growth, like galls on trees, or elephantiasis of the navel, or a huge bunion' (117). Clara has been '. . . dragged slowly down into the gigantic pumpkin-like growth that was enveloping her body' (117). Given the recurrence of the pumpkin as an image of pregnancy, it is small wonder that Marian ultimately rejects Peter, whose name and character recall the nursery rhyme about the Pumpkin-Eater, and regards Duncan with suspicion when he is seen to have been consuming large numbers of pumpkin seeds. As Marian flees the maternity ward where Clara has finally given birth, she has 'the sense of having escaped, as if from a culvert or cave' (135).

Ainsley, Marian's at least theoretically liberated roommate, next decides to make her contribution to society in the form of a super-baby (perhaps 'the Great Canadian Baby' itself which Atwood discusses in *Survival*) which she plans to raise without the inhibiting effects of paternal influence. When Marian learns that the baby has been conceived in *her* bed, the situation becomes doubly threatening, undoubtedly because she feels somehow implicated, involved in a process which repels her. Marian shares the prospective father's disgust at Ainsley's announcement; Len waves his beer-bottle and laments, 'Now I'm going to be all mentally tangled up in Birth. Fecundity. Gestation. Don't you realize what that will do to me? It's obscene, that horrible oozy . . .' (163). Len attributes his phobic reaction to a traumatic incident in childhood in which his mother forced him to eat an egg which he was convinced contained an unborn chicken: '. . . there was a little beak and little claws and everything' (164). Marian's next experience with an egg is predictable: '. . . she opened her soft-boiled egg and saw the yolk looking up at her with its one significant and accusing yellow eye' (165). Alice as a serpent, according to Fish, was also 'hostile to eggs', that obvious symbol of maternity complicated by distinct suggestions of cannibalism.

Talk of future parenthood precedes Marian's first attack of anorexia. She and Peter are eating steak in a restaurant (much of the novel is set in restaurants or kitchens, and much of the action and imagery involve mouths and the process of eating, as is also the case in the *Alice* books) when Marian visualises her meat as that most maternal of creatures, a cow, first as the kind of cow pictured in cook books with the lines drawn to indicate the cuts, and then as the living animal, 'flesh and blood, rare, and she had been devouring it. Gorging herself on it' (155). Soon Marian is unable to eat anything but salads, and even carrots begin to take on a kind of life. The very mould growing on the accumulating dirty dishes in her kitchen has, she believes, as much right to life as she has. But it is not a respect for life which prevents Marian from eating; in fact, the opposite is true. Life disgusts her, as do the functions of living; she watches her female coworkers eating, and she is simultaneously fascinated and repelled by '. . . the continual flux between the outside and the inside, taking things in, giving them out, chewing, words, potato chips, burps, grease, hair, babies, milk, excrement, cookies, vomit, coffee, tomato-juice, blood . . . she felt suffocated by this thick sargasso-sea of femininity'. Claustrophobia ensues, as is the case when Marian visits Clara in the maternity ward, and she wants only to escape this 'sweet organic scent' and to place 'a fixed barrier between herself and that liquid amorphous other' (172).

Psychiatric explanations for anorexia are, of course, complex, but Atwood does in this novel prefigure a great many current theories: in one sense, Marian's antipathy to food is clearly a rejection of her female identity and the maternity that identity seems to her inevitably to imply. Pregnancy, like food, makes one fat, but it also represents a loss of autonomy, an alien presence in one's own body which directs action, in effect, takes over. Just as Alice underground cannot control what effects on her body the various substances she ingests will have ('Eat Me', 'Drink Me', but there is no warning label as to whether she will grow or shrink and with what dire consequences), so Marian is 'afraid of losing her shape, spreading out, not being able to contain herself any longer' (225). Marian fears this loss of control, which is both physical and emotional, and, in fact, her life and her future *are* out of her control, subject to role prescriptions and the desires of others. Her only autonomy, she feels, is to direct what she will eat or not eat. Such eating disorders symbolic of role rejection are also frequent images in Atwood's later fiction: Joan Foster in *Lady Oracle*, for example, can manipulate her world only by changing the size of her body. By eating a very great deal, Joan can separate herself from her domineering mother by refusing to resemble her; in this way she rejects not only her individual mother but the maternal role in general. The motivation behind anorexia, a disease which Atwood sees as so problematic in young women, is not so much a desire for fashionable slimness, as an attempt to avoid womanhood, to remain a little girl, in essence to escape one's very humanity.

Yet another means of escaping one's humanity is, simply, to abdicate, to think of one's self in terms of a child, an animal, or even of an inanimate object. Marian's anorexia is also clearly linked with her vision of herself as an animal, a prey to the male hunter in the person of Peter. Her own victimisation is thus mirrored in the sacrificial deaths of animals for food. Atwood writes in *Survival* about animal victims as a theme in Canadian literature, and theorises that 'the English Canadian projects himself through his animal images as a threatened victim' (*Survival*, 80). Certainly, as we will see in Chapter 3, the protagonist of *Surfacing* sees her own victimisation as symbolised by the crucified heron, even in the fish she herself kills for food. For Marian in *The Edible Woman*, the primary identification is with rabbits, not for their legendary fertility, but for their vulnerability. She listens while Peter describes a hunting incident to Len, man-to-man:

> So I let her off and Wham. One shot, right through
> the heart . . . I picked it up and Trigger said,
> "You know how to gut them, you just slit her down

the belly and give her a good hard shake and all the
guts'll fall out." So I whipped out my knife, good
knife, German steel, and slit the belly and took her
by the hind legs and gave her one hell of a crack, like
a whip you see, and the next thing you know there
was blood and guts all over the place. All over me,
what a mess, rabbit guts dangling from the trees,
god the trees were red for yards. . . . (70)

Peter and his friend 'Trigger' then proceed to take 'shots'
of the 'whole mess' with a camera, an instrument Atwood
frequently associates with guns or with psychological
annihilation. In her poem 'Camera', for example, Atwood
transforms the mechanical object into an instrument of a
lover's manipulation: 'How can I love your glass eye?' the
speaker asks (*Circle Game*, 56). In 'This is a Photograph of
Me', the 'drowned' speaker identifies her presence in the
photograph as 'in the lake, under the center/of the
picture, just under the surface' (*Circle Game*, 17), and the
implication is that the photograph itself rather than the
lake is responsible for her drowning. We will see in the
next chapter that the movie camera in *Surfacing* functions
as a device for torture, an instrument for symbolic rape.
Peter, too, is a camera enthusiast and it is his insistence
on 'getting a shot' at Marian later in the novel which
precipitates her final flight.

   Shortly after Peter's account of his hunting expedition,
Marian begins to withdraw, even physically to the point
that she hides beneath a bed in Len's apartment while the
conversation continues above her: 'I was thinking of the
room as "up there". I myself was underground, I had dug
myself a private burrow' (77). Marian's bizarre behaviour
is somehow attractive to Peter, and the evening ends with
his proposal of marriage and her acceptance, although, in
the flash of lightning which ominously accompanies his
proposal, she sees herself 'small and oval, mirrored in his

eyes' (84). Following the engagement, Marian finds herself unable to eat anything but salad: 'She felt like a rabbit, crunching all the time on mounds of leafy greenery' (178). Her final escape from Peter on the night of their engagement party is a kind of nightmare flight, a rabbit's terror, combined with the surreal imagery and claustrophic paranoia encountered so frequently in the *Alice* books:

> It had been a long search. She retraced through time the corridors and rooms, long corridors, large rooms. Everything seemed to be slowing down . . . . She opened the door to the right and went in. There was Peter, forty-five and balding but still recognizable as Peter, standing in bright sunlight beside a barbecue with a long fork in his hand . . . . She looked carefully for herself in the garden, but she wasn't there . . . . No, she thought, this has to be the wrong room. It can't be the last one. And now she could see there was another door, in the hedge at the other side of the garden . . . . She was back in Peter's living room with the people and the noise . . . except that people seemed even clearer now, more sharply focused, further away, and they were moving faster and faster . . . . She ran for the next door, yanked it open. Peter was there, dressed in his dark opulent winter suit. He had a camera in his hand . . . . (250)

Marian has projected the image of Peter as hunter from the beginning of the novel. Under the facade of the impeccably-dressed young lawyer and prospective husband, Marian finds the heart of a killer, a reader of detective novels, a collector of guns and cameras, even the possibility of perversion as 'the Underwear Man', that anonymous male voice reputed to telephone women in order to learn their preference in intimate garments. Marian's own market survey which she conducts as part of her job at Seymour Surveys is an analogous invasion of privacy, though she does not realise this. She searches for male reactions to a beer commercial, a commercial designed to appeal to the male as hunter, to elicit the 'mystical identity with the plaid-jacketed sportsman shown in the pictures with his foot on a deer or scooping a trout into his net' (25). Marian thus divides her world by establishing polarities between the male and female psyche, between the hunter and the hunted, eater and eaten, victor and victim, consumer and consumed. Marian is like the speaker in 'A Descent Through the Carpet' who moves into a womb-like watery world to find 'cold jewelled symmetries' and yet 'total fear' in the form of sea creatures which represent 'the voracious eater/the voracious eaten' (*Circle Game*, 30). Such divisions allow Marian to regard herself as powerless, as innocent, as child-like or even animal-like. She cannot eat or love or marry Peter or have a baby or write a poem, because these activities would force a recognition of her own humanity and the guilt thereby implicit. Like the protagonist of *Surfacing*, Marian 'refuses to be human'.

Critic Nina Auerbach in *Romantic Imprisonment* argues in similar terms about the innocence versus the guilt of Lewis Carroll's Alice. According to Auerbach, Alice herself projects 'the bizarre anarchy of her dream country . . . . The sea that almost drowns her is composed of her own tears, and the dream that nearly obliterates her is composed of fragments of her own personality'.[1] Alice thus is both eater and eaten, writes Auerbach, and this is symbolised in the final banquet in *Through the Looking Glass* as 'the food comes alive and begins to eat the guests'.[2] Auerbach sees that 'the core of Alice's nature . . . seems to lie in her mouth: the eating and drinking that direct her size changes and motivate much of her behavior, the songs and verses that pop out of her inadvertently, all are involved with things entering and leaving her mouth'.[3] The 'demonic

Alice', the cannibalistic 'hungry Alice', are images juxtaposed to the model of Victorian childhood and innocence, and they indicate, according to Auerbach, Carroll's concerns about Original Sin. Alice and the Rabbit, the girl and the animal, Auerbach contends, are but aspects of one self, 'looking glass versions of each other'.[4]

While it is not likely that Atwood is concerned with Original Sin in any theological sense, she is certainly concerned with the tendency of women to reject their human capacities and to insist on their own innocence. Mutual guilt for victimisation is a recurrent theme in Atwood's poetry as well as in her novels. Both men and women are losers in the struggle for power which is the subject of much of her poetry including *Power Politics*: 'Next time we commit/love, we ought to/choose in advance what to kill' (35). For Atwood, brutality feeds on vulnerability, and the horrible is juxtaposed to the commonplace: 'You fit into me/like a hook into an eye/a fish hook/an open eye' (*Power Politics*, 1). In 'They Eat Out', it is the woman's fantasy of murder and mutilation which is recounted; it is she who is the eater and killer, and yet her victim is somehow triumphant in the end: 'I raise the magic fork/over the plate of beef fried rice/and plunge it into your heart./There is a faint pop, a sizzle/and through your own split head/you rise up glowing' (*Power Politics*, 5). The symbolic hunter and the hunted are in reality one identity, as Atwood writes in 'A Pursuit': 'Through the wilderness of the flesh/across the mind's ice/expanses, we hunt each other. . . . Through the tangle of each other/we hunt ourselves' (*The Animals in That Country*, 66–67). So also, as in Canadian folk tradition, the actual hunter and his animal prey are aspects of each other: in 'The Trappers', Atwood writes, 'I can understand/the guilt they feel because/they are not animals/the guilt they feel/because they are' (*The Animals in That Country*, 35). According to Sherrill Grace in *Violent Duality*, Atwood's primary concern is our insistence on dividing the world into polarities; thus we subvert the 'underlying unity in life': 'Atwood implies that subject and object are one, that by polarizing them we *create* power and suffering.'[5]

Certainly Marian in *The Edible Woman* is held largely responsible for the projection of her world; the guilt that is inherent there is a reflection of her own human guilt, given Atwood's system of justice. If, as Marian illogically suspects, Peter is the infamous Underwear Man, this is only because Marian is also somehow perverted. Atwood frequently uses the image of the killer or the rapist as a reflection or mirror image of the victim. In a poem called 'The Green Man; For the Boston Strangler', for example, Atwood writes: 'He turned toward them/his face, a clear mirror . . . . In it they saw reflected their/own sanity' (*The Animals in That Country*, 12). Similarly, in a review of Erica Jong's poetry, Atwood discusses Jong's 'sexual gothic figure' in 'The Man Under the Bed': 'He is Death, sinister and frightening, but he is also a lover and attractive; he is the lure of suicide, and he is thus created by the poet herself' (*Second Words*, 170).

As Marian in *The Edible Woman* creates a sinister aspect of Peter, she also projects a purely subjective reality for the other characters in the novel: her women coworkers are perceived as caged armadillos, '. . . going around in figure-eights, just around and around in the same path' (98); her landlady, 'the lady down below', is surely a kind of Queen of Hearts who would gladly decapitate the young men who visit. She is a force for propriety, like the character in Atwood's poem, 'The Landlady', who is 'solid as bacon', 'a slab of what is real' (*The Animals in That Country*, 15). Marian's world, and all the people in it, are thus reflections of herself, projections of her own disturbed and immature psyche.

The most complexly symbolic of Marian's friends is Duncan, combination Rabbit-guide and Mock-Turtle, who

serves as Marian's double. Early in the novel, Marian puts
on Duncan's dressing gown, and he comments that she
looks exactly like him. Duncan is, in fact, Marian's anorexic
and hungry self, 'a starved buddha burning incense to
itself' (51), eating seeds meant for birds, 'his spare body,
the gaunt slope of a starved animal in time of famine'
(176). Acting as a link between Marian's fantasy world and
her real one, he appears mysteriously in illogical places
where Marian least expects him. 'But really', he says, 'I'm
not human at all, I come from the underground' (144).
Like the Mock-Turtle in Fish's analysis of *Alice*, and like
Marian herself, Duncan is full of self-pity; he and Marian,
in fact, exploit each other shamelessly in the matter of
comparing pain to see who suffers more and thus deserves
the greater sympathy: 'You shouldn't expect me to do
anything,' Duncan tells Marian, 'I want to go back to my
shell. . . . You aren't an escape any more, you're too
real' (265). Duncan's androgynous personality cannot
accommodate sex and sexuality any more than Marian can.
Most of their relationship is asexual, just as Marian would
also prefer. When Marian decides, however, that it is her
role to force the issue, both the setting and the act are a
grotesque parody. The hotel is a sleazy place renting rooms
by the hour, Marian is dressed in gaudy red suggesting the
costume of a prostitute, and Duncan's first attempts at
sex result in impotence: 'I feel like some kind of little
stunted creature crawling over the surface of a huge
mass of flesh', he explains. 'Not that you're fat . . . you
aren't. There's just altogether too much flesh around here.
It's suffocating' (261). Again, Marian's own claustrophobia
in relation to femaleness is evoked.

Duncan is not only sexless, but ageless as well. He is not
merely adolescent, like the Mock-Turtle of Fish's analysis,
but infantile. His roommates are surrogate parents who
feed him one moment and scold him the next: 'I've been
running away from understudy mothers ever since I can

remember', Duncan tells Marian; '. . . that's what you get
for being an orphan' (143). At times Marian too must
struggle against the temptation to mother Duncan, to kiss
his wounds: 'you need me' (247), she tells him on the night
of their sexual encounter. Their first kiss takes place in the
'Mummy Room' of the Royal Ontario Museum where
Duncan introduces Marian to his 'womb symbol', the
skeleton of a child in a fetal pose: 'with its jutting ribs and
frail legs and starved shoulder-blades it looked like the
photographs of people from underprivileged countries or
concentration camps' (193). The preserved child is Duncan's
image of himself, but it is also an image of the self for
Marian. Duncan is not Marian's surrogate baby, but her
*self* as baby. When Duncan finally begins to assume a
sexual role in the hotel room, it is Marian who responds by
curling into a fetal position. Neither is in an emotional
position to 'GIVE THE GIFT OF LIFE', an advertisement
Marian notices on the bus one day. The slogan accompanies
the photograph of a nurse, crisp and competent; from the
beginning of their relationship, Marian has considered that
she ought to approach Duncan as a kind of patient: 'The
situation, she thought, called for stout shoes and starched
cuffs and a leather bag full of hypodermic needles' (195).
By the end of the novel, however, Marian recognises the
manipulative aspects of such an approach: 'the starched
nurse-like image of herself she had tried to preserve as a
last resort crumpled like wet newsprint' (271). Duncan has
warned Marian earlier that 'I bring out the Florence
Nightingale' in women. He recognises the paradox that to
nurse is to render the receiver either infantile or invalid;
therefore Marian should beware: 'You might do something
destructive: hunger is more basic than love. Florence
Nightingale was a cannibal, you know' (102).

Duncan may be a projection of Marian's self, but he is
also her alter-ego: he does point directions; he ultimately
leads her to some form of understanding and frees her

from her self, or at least from her sense of her self as either
nurse or victim. On the morning after Marian's engagement
party and her night in the hotel with Duncan, he conducts
her through the twisted maze of Toronto's streets and
ravines and brings her finally to a great open pit, a 'gigantic
hole scooped into the ground' (270). Together, they sit in
the snow at the edge of the abyss, which looks like
nothingness, like absence, like death, perhaps. 'It's your
own personal cul-de-sac', Duncan tells Marian, 'you
invented it, you'll have to think of your own way out'
(272). With this exhortation to responsibility, Marian leaves
the ravine, the pit, the burrow, the underground, and
moves back to the street alone, towards reality and,
perhaps, out of her Alice existence. Duncan remains
behind, '. . . a dark shape against the snow, crouched on
the edge and gazing into the empty pit' (272).

Following these events, several abrupt changes take
place. The narrative returns to first person, as it was in the
beginning of the novel, which indicates a quality of self-
direction, of autonomy. Marian returns to her apartment,
takes off the red sequined dress which had made her such a
good 'target' for Peter, washes her dishes, restores order in
general, and proceeds to bake a cake, an elaborate cake cut
and decorated to look like a woman in a bright pink ruffled
dress wearing her hair in 'intricate baroque scrolls and
swirls', just as Marian had worn hers to her engagement
party. 'Her creation gazed up at her, its face doll-like and
vacant except for the small silver glitter of intelligence in
each green eye . . . "You look delicious," she told her . . .
"And that's what will happen to you; that's what you get
for being food"' (277–78). The cake is, of course, an effigy
of Marian's self and of her identity as a consumable item in
a consumer society. She invites Peter to partake: 'You've
been trying to destroy me, haven't you. . . . You've been
trying to assimilate me. But I've made you a substitute,
something you'll like much better' (279). Peter is horrified

and leaves Marian to eat the cake alone, which she does
with great relish, spearing chunks of pink thigh and
plunging her fork 'into the carcass, neatly severing the
body from the head' (280). Duncan, however, is willing to
share in Marian's self-cannibalism, and he sees in the cake
the symbolic significance Marian intended, although he
indicates that her motives are mistaken: 'Peter wasn't
trying to destroy you', he tells Marian, 'That's just
something you made up. Actually you were trying to
destroy him' (287).

Perhaps there are as many interpretations of Marian's
symbolic cake and of the ending of *The Edible Woman* as
there are readers. According to Robert Lecker in 'Janus
through the Looking Glass', Marian has been from the
beginning a 'packaged product of a male-dominated
corporate society', and her rejection of food 'is synonymous
with her rejection of a culture which tends to exploit
women and treat them as edible objects'. Her final act of
eating the cake, according to Lecker, is a form of
reconciliation, a recognition that she is herself 'a mixture of
consumer and consumed'.[6] For Catherine McLay in 'The
Dark Voyage: *The Edible Woman* as Romance', Marian's
cake represents a 'feast, the celebration of Marian's new
freedom and even rebirth . . .'. She is 'released from the
spell, from her identification of herself with the victim. No
longer isolated and alien, Marian has rejoined society'.[7]
Kim Chernin in *The Obsession: Reflections on the Tyranny of
Slenderness* sees the final scenes in *The Edible Woman* as
even more highly symbolic: 'By eating up this cake fetish
of a woman's body she assimilates for the first time her
own body and its feelings. It is a re-enactment of the ritual
feast, in which the eating of an animal's flesh, or a piece of
cake shaped like a breast, signifies the coming together of
human and divine, individual with collective . . . a woman
with her own body and feelings'.[8]

Atwood herself, however, is not so optimistic about the

conclusion of *The Edible Woman*: '. . . in the end it's more pessimistic than *Surfacing*. The difference between them is that *The Edible Woman* is a circle and *Surfacing* is a spiral . . . the heroine of *Surfacing* does not end where she began'.[9] And, in *Second Words*, Atwood remarks, '. . . my heroine's choices remain much the same at the end of the book as they are at the beginning: career going nowhere, or marriage as an exit from it' (370). Perhaps the cake and the self-cannibalism it symbolises are but another of Atwood's 'self-indulgent grotesqueries', as she herself has characterised certain of her images in the novel (*Second Words*, 369). Certainly, Atwood has incorporated every relevant fairy tale into the elaborate detective game which is this novel. (Even *Goldilocks and the Three Bears* is invoked at that point when Marian first enters Duncan's apartment and tries out all the various chairs. Goldilocks, too, is a consumer, an eater of other people's porridge.) Surely Atwood would not be so remiss as to ignore other examples of cannibalism in fairy tales, like those Duncan cites as a pattern: '. . . the husband kills the wife's lover, or vice versa, and cuts out the heart and makes it into a stew or a pie and serves it up in a silver dish, and the other one eats it' (53). No matter how desperately the reader seeks for heroism in this novel, Atwood will not permit our private mythologies to contradict her ironic humour.

Nevertheless, we are tempted to argue with Atwood about the ending of *The Edible Woman*, that surely Marian knows more than she did in the beginning; if she is not, in fact, celebrating the unity of the 'human and the divine' or has not changed either her society or her own social condition, at least she has come to terms with something, has objectified her situation and apprehended it more realistically. The cake thus serves as a reflection, a way of seeing herself as in a mirror, and it expresses a truth not before perceived. The cake is 'doll-like', and Marian has previously conceived of herself as a kind of doll. On the night of her engagement party, she looks into a mirror at herself in the flamboyant red dress, her hair elaborately done, the make-up forming a mask: 'She held both of her naked arms out towards the mirror. They were the only portion of her flesh that was without a cloth or nylon or leather or varnish covering, but in the glass even they looked fake, like soft pinkish-white rubber or plastic, boneless, flexible . . .' (235). Another mirror scene just previous to this one is also associated with dolls, the actual ones that Marian has retained since her childhood and which represent another indication that she has refused to grow up. The two dolls, one blonde and one dark, are also symbolic of Marian's two-sided and split self, the result of her insistence on dividing the world into polarities of light and dark, eaten and eater, good and evil. The dolls regard her accusingly:

> She saw herself in the mirror between them for an instant as though she was inside them, inside both of them at once, looking out . . . the two overlapping images drawing further and further away from each other; the centre, whatever it was in the glass, the thing that held them together, would soon be quite empty. By the strength of their separate visions they were trying to pull her apart. (225–226)

In 'Five Poems for Dolls', Atwood reiterates this image of dolls as self-projections, as embodiments of the speaker's own guilt: 'see how the dolls resent us/with their bulging foreheads/and minimal chins. This is not a smile,/this glossy mouth/two stunted teeth;/the dolls gaze at us/with the filmed eyes of killers' (*Two-Headed Poems*, 17). But perhaps, the poems continue, dolls represent our guilt because they are our unborn children: '. . . all dolls come/from the land of the unborn,/the almost-born; each/doll is a future/dead at the roots' (*Two-Headed Poems*,

20). Atwood's 'doll' poems recall T. S. Eliot's image of the rose garden which is the land of unborn children, and also, by extension, Alice's vision of the tiny rose garden from which she is excluded by her size. In *Surfacing* also, the mutilated doll left to drown in the lake is a prefiguration of the protagonist's abortion and of her own self-victimisation. In *The Edible Woman*, Marian's cake also functions as a doll, a representation of Marian herself as both doll and infant, but it is also perhaps her symbolic child, an indication of her recognition if not her acceptance of her identity as 'Woman'. When Ainsley exclaims with horror, 'You're rejecting your femininity!' (280), she is correct in her observation, but wrong in her interpretation. Marian does indeed reject the childish and doll-like femininity of her former self, but in order to affirm the adult woman, the human being the reader can at least hope she has become.

The cake also clearly represents Marian's one truly creative act. Like all of Atwood's heroines, Marian is a frustrated artist, a writer who doesn't write. She has rejected or denied her own creative possibilities by becoming a 'manipulator of words' at Seymour Surveys ('see-more'?). Her rejection of the maternal role is consummate with her rejection of creativity in general. Fish again provides the clue to the validity of the theme recurrent in Atwood's work that artistic creativity is symbolically analogous to giving birth:

> And so then consequently the poet also thought of himself as the same kind of natural producer; his poem was something begotten so to speak on him by the Muses, or let's say maybe Apollo, hence the term 'inspiration,' the instilling of breath as it were into, the poet was pregnant with his work, the poem went through a period of gestation, often a long one, and when it was finally ready to see the light of day

the poet was delivered of it often with much painful
labor. In this way the very process of artistic
creation was itself an imitation of Nature, of the
thing in nature that was most important to the
survival of Mankind. I mean birth; birth. (203–204)

Fish is of course pontificating as usual, but, in the end, we
must believe that his is a version of truth. Ultimately, Fish
takes his place in Atwood's parodic version of the Holy
Family as surrogate father, a Joseph figure, to Ainsley's
unborn baby. But Marian will not, we must assume,
deliver herself of *The Edible Woman*, nor will she come to
embody Fish's ideal of the creative spirit as 'a new Venus,
big-bellied, teeming with life, potential, about to give birth
to a new world in all its plenitude, a new Venus rising from
the sea' (205). Of the female literary stereotypes Atwood
discusses in *Survival*, Marian will remain a Diana rather
than become a Venus. But she has at least graduated from
her Alice phase, and she has learned a great deal about life
and the processes of living, about being human. For Atwood
as for the reader, such recognition is a form of heroism.
Marian, finally, is like the speaker in Atwood's poem, 'All
Bread', who urges a reconciliation between innocence and
guilt: 'Lift these ashes/into your mouth, your blood;/to
know what you devour/is to consecrate it,/almost. All
bread must be broken/so it can be shared. Together/we
eat this earth' (*Two-Headed Poems*, 108).

# 3 'Border Country': *Surfacing* and *The Journals of Susanna Moodie*

'This is border country' (30), the nameless protagonist of *Surfacing* reminds herself as she journeys toward her childhood home in the wilderness of northern Canada. She means that she is on the border between English and French Canada, that division of a country which Atwood sees in *The Journals of Susanna Moodie* and in *Survival* as a manifestation of a national schizophrenia. But, like Susanna Moodie who is her spiritual ancestor, the protagonist has spent most of her life in metaphorical 'border country', maintaining a precarious balance between truth and lies, between reality and fantasy, between sanity and utter derangement. And, *Surfacing*, more than any other of Atwood's novels, is also 'border country', halfway between poem and novel, theological treatise and political manifesto, myth and realism. Unlike that of her protagonist, Atwood's balance between generic worlds is almost perfect, and *Surfacing* is, quite possibly, the best of all her work.

Like all of Atwood's poetry and fiction including *The Edible Woman*, *Surfacing* can be read on a series of levels, the most superficial but still entertaining of which is the detective story. In recognisable Nancy Drew style, the protagonist in this novel sets out from the city, accompanied by three friends, to solve the mystery of her scientist father's disappearance. They search for clues on the remote island where the protagonist spent much of her childhood and where the father has lived alone since the death of his wife some years earlier. Possible solutions to the mystery are that the father has been murdered by avaricious Americans who want his land for a hunting lodge, that he has committed suicide, or that he is alive but insane, 'bushed' by living in the wilderness too long alone. None of the above provides the answer, and the sense of menace grows along with the protagonist's recognition that the island itself is treacherous, perhaps even haunted. The mystery is solved only when the protagonist, using the enigmatic maps and 'pictographs' left by her father, finds his drowned body in the lake, weighted down and prevented from 'surfacing' by the camera he used to photograph underwater cave paintings of ancient Indians. The 'ghosts' of both her mother and father appear briefly to the protagonist, and, the mystery resolved, she packs up to go home to the city.

But, again, this is 'border country': nothing is definite. There are no solutions to the real mystery with which Atwood presents us, which is the identity of the protagonist and the reliability of her narrative. Atwood has remarked in an interview that *Surfacing* is a 'ghost story', '. . . the Henry James kind, in which the ghost that one sees is in fact a fragment of one's own self which has split off, and that to me is the most interesting and that is obviously the tradition I'm working in'.[1] James's *Turn of the Screw*, to which Atwood refers, is, like many other great mystery stories including those of Edgar Allen Poe, dependent for its quality of horror on the psychopathology of the narrator rather than on any manifestation of the supernatural. Atwood's narrator is similarly undependable, perhaps mad; certainly the reader

cannot trust her judgement, based as it is on the lies, the
'alibis', that she tells both the reader and herself. The ghost
in this novel finally is the protagonist's self: she is a
psychological suicide, a woman with no name, an artist with
no art form and no past or tradition that she can recall
correctly. She can neither 'feel' nor communicate effectively.
She has a lover she cannot love; she is a mother without a
child, and a child without a mother.

From the beginning of the novel Atwood provides
indications that her narrator cannot be trusted, that she has
somehow lost touch with the reality of her own life: 'I have
to be more careful about my memories', she says, 'I have to
be sure they're my own. . . . I run quickly over my version
of it, my life, checking it like an alibi' (84). One of the lies
that the protagonist tells the reader, her friends and her
lover, and even herself is that she is divorced and the
mother of a young child who lives with the former husband.
What she and we learn as the novel progresses, however, is
that she was never married, but rather involved with her
married art teacher who gave her C's in his class, told her
there were no great women artists and insisted she have an
abortion rather than disrupt his life with her pregnancy.
Only after the trauma of discovering her father's body in
the lake, 'a dark oval trailing limbs' (167), does the
protagonist connect with the other 'something I knew
about, a dead thing' (167) which is her aborted baby: 'I
knew when it was, it was in a bottle curled up, staring out
at me like a cat pickled . . . it had drowned in air . . .
whatever it is, part of myself or a separate creature, I killed
it. It wasn't a child but it could have been one, I didn't
allow it' (168). Like a criminal pleading innocence, the
protagonist creates an alibi to avoid the inevitable
confrontation with her own guilt.

As she begins to recognise her complicity in the abortion,
so the protagonist must also recognise that she has killed
yet another and analogous part of herself. Given Atwood's

frequent use of the archetypal fertility myth and her association of artistic creativity with procreation as was discussed in earlier chapters, it is not surprising that the protagonist of *Surfacing* is also, like all of Atwood's other heroines, a failed artist as well as a failed mother: 'I'm what they call a commercial artist, or, when the job is more pretentious, an illustrator. . . . I can imitate anything: fake Walt Disney, Victorian etchings in sepia, Bavarian cookies, ersatz Eskimo for the home market' (60–61). Her current project is the illustration of a volume of fairy tales for children, but she is not as successful at imitation as she would have us believe. Her princesses look like the vapid movie-star paper dolls she created as a child, 'sausage rolls of hair across their foreheads, with puffed red mouths and eyelashes like toothbrush bristles' (49), and the evil giants who pursue them resemble nothing more ominous than lumpy football players. The fairy tale she invents on paper, then, is as unsuccessful as the fairy-tale alibi she invents for her life. In thus betraying her talent through compromise, choosing to be an illustrator rather than an artist, putting her career in a 'samsonite case', the protagonist fails in her responsibility to herself as much as if she had committed suicide: both her art and her aborted baby represent 'A section of my own life, sliced off from me like a Siamese twin, my own flesh cancelled' (56).

The protagonist's lover, Joe, and his friend David, are also failed artists, the film they are making on the way to the island a parody of art. 'Random Samples' depends for its effects on that which is degraded or bizarre in Canada and in human nature: the stuffed moose family on the restaurant roof, the house made of coke bottles, the WELCOME sign with the bullet holes, the carcasses of dead animals, and the naked body of Anna, David's wife. To work with cameras, given Atwood's recurrent symbolism, is to cheat at art, to fail at *seeing*, to exploit the natural, perhaps even to 'steal not only your soul but your body also' (139). Certainly that is David's motive and his perversion of art as he trains his phallic movie camera on his wife's naked body like 'a bazooka or a strange instrument of torture' (160). One certain sign which Atwood provides of the protagonist's ultimate regeneration is her act of destroying the false art, stealing the film and throwing it into the lake, that symbol of both life and death which, we know from early in the novel, is 'blue and cool as redemption' (18).

The protagonist cannot, however, redeem Anna, who is also a failed artist of sorts, practising her craft before a mirror where she carefully applies the cosmetic camouflage so necessary to her in the war of sexual politics in which she is engaged with her husband. Anna's soul, the protagonist imagines, is 'closed in the gold compact, that and not the camera is what I should have broken' (205). Anna, an older and more debased version of Ainsley, the roommate in *The Edible Woman*, is also a princess in flight, a parody of a fairy tale, an incarnation of the evil queen in 'Snow White' who sits before her mirror but never asks the fatal questions: '. . . pink on the cheeks and black discreetly around the eyes, as red as blood as black as ebony, a seamed and folded imitation of a magazine picture that is itself an imitation of a woman who also is an imitation . . . captive princess in someone's head' (194). Anna, too, is childless, a slave to the technology of birth control pills and the violation of both nature and art they imply in Atwood's symbolic scheme. The pills, in fact, function like the camera, that other product of technology, in that they too, according to the protagonist's experience, have the side effect of obscuring and distorting vision, 'like having a film of vasoline on my eyes' (95). Anna, however, does not need to see; she is not an artist but an object of art, the product of artifice as much as if she had stepped from the pages of the scrapbooks of the protagonist's childhood pictures of 'ladies'.

In spite of his participation in the creation of 'Random Samples', Joe is in one sense a better artist than any of the others, including the protagonist. His squashed ceramic pots, unsold and unusable, litter their apartment in the city; he too is a failure, but at least he does not compromise, he does not opt for the commercial or the expedient. Joe does not tell lies with art or reduce it to artifice. 'Perhaps it's not only his body I like', the protagonist recognises, 'perhaps it's his failure; that also has a kind of purity' (67). Atwood then is highly moral in this novel as in others about what function art ought to fulfil, whether on the personal level or on the political level. Whether art is perversion or idealism, whether it is the protagonist's childhood drawings of 'ladies' and movie stars or the equally child-like cave drawings of the ancient Indians her father died in discovering, it represents a key to understanding individual and cultural identity: 'You draw on the wall what's important to you, what you're hunting' (142).

In preserving her children's drawings in volumes of scrapbooks, the protagonist's mother has, in essence, given them their past. Having destroyed her own past, the protagonist is sorely in need of such a 'gift' from her mother, for the drawings are a key to her own identity, a 'pictograph'. She looks first at the scrapbook containing her brother's drawings and discovers there what she perceives as quintessential masculinity: 'explosions in red and orange, soldiers dismembering in the air, planes and tanks . . . little swastikas on the sides. . . . a man-eating plant, engulfing a careless victim, a balloon with HELP in it squeezing out of his mouth like bubble gum' (108). The protagonist's own drawings, those that precede the movie stars, are, in contrast, expressions of an innocent femininity: 'Page after page of eggs and rabbits, grass and trees, normal and green, surrounding them, flowers blooming, sun in the upper right-hand corner of each picture, moon

symmetrically in the left. . . . No monsters, no wars, no
explosions, no heroism . . . perhaps it was a vision of
Heaven' (109–10). The protagonist begins the process of
recalling her vision of herself, for art does indeed represent
'what you're hunting'. She recalls her sense of herself as
good and innocent: remaining aloof or repairing the
damages of cruelty perpetrated by her brother, freeing the
insects he had imprisoned in bottles and then forgotten,
suffering while he threw 'the bad kind' of leeches on the
campfire where they sizzled and smoked and writhed.
Sometimes, the protagonist herself was the animal-victim,
tied to a tree in the school yard by boys who ran away and
forgot her: 'I became an escape artist of sorts, expert at
undoing knots' (83).

But sometimes, the protagonist begins to remember, she
lost her innocence, was not merely a victim but an actual
participant in the games of cruelty. No person, adult or
child, male or female, is truly innocent in Atwood's literary
world, and perhaps especially not children: 'To become a
little child again, a barbarian, a vandal; it was in us too, it
was innate' (156). At one point, the protagonist recalls, she
and her brother collaborated in a kind of murder:

> . . . we killed other people besides Hitler, before my
> brother went to school and learned about him and
> the games became war games. Earlier we would play
> we were animals; our parents were the humans, the
> enemies who might shoot us or catch us, we would
> hide from them. But sometimes the animals had
> power too: one time we were a swarm of bees, we
> gnawed the fingers, feet and nose off our least
> favorite doll, ripped her cloth body open and pulled
> out the stuffing, it was gray and fluffy like the insides
> of mattresses; then we threw her body into the
> lake. . . . Of course the doll wasn't hurt, it wasn't
> alive; though children think everything is alive. (154).

This passage prefigures the protagonist's complicity in the abortion, one of the acts for which she must accept responsibility before she can regain her identity and assume her humanity.

But the protagonist is 'an escape artist of sorts' and 'expert at undoing knots' (83), except for the psychological knots in which she finds herself so tied and bound. The primary escape route is through thinking of herself as victim, but she also depends for psychological survival on a kind of passive aggression: she becomes 'invisible'. The protagonist recalls that, on being introduced to Christianity and the idea of prayer when she was a child, she prayed 'for something real. I prayed to be made invisible, and when in the morning everyone could still see me I knew they had the wrong God' (84). If, in fact, the world is divided cleanly between good and evil, victim and victor, princesses and giants, as the protagonist continues to see it, then one can choose simply to abdicate, refuse to participate or take sides, cease to be visible or even to exist: 'There were only two things you could be, a winner or a loser . . . they couldn't figuure out what to do about me since I wouldn't play' (82). The heroine at this point is still not playing, still opting for the third alternative of non-existence: remaining in 'border country'. She refuses to 'feel' and thus protects herself from pain: 'Anesthesia, that's one technique' (15). She also finds herself unable to communicate, identifying with deaf and dumb children she imagines to be locked away in rooms and never taught a language as part of some inhumane scientific experiment; language, she says 'divides us into fragments' (172). The very style in which her first-person narrative is delivered is fragmented, unemotional, reportorial.

She is thus totally isolated from her friends who are not really her friends, because she prevents such a relationship. She has known Anna only two months, yet she is 'my best woman friend' (12). Even her relationship with Joe is characterised by this same refusal to feel or to commit herself in any real sense. She lives with him because he asked her to: 'It wasn't even a real decision, it was more like buying a goldfish or a potted cactus plant, not because you want one in advance but because you happen to be in the store and you see them lined up on the counter' (49). She ponders the benefits of sex between two people with paper bags over their heads; she considers the possibility of sticking pins in her arms because even 'rats prefer any sensation to none' (133). 'I rehearsed emotions, naming them: joy, peace, guilt, love and hate, react, relate; what to feel was like what to wear, you watched the others and memorized it. But the only thing there was the fear that I wasn't alive: a negative . . .' (132).

The state of being a 'negative' is also a desirable condition of life for the mad heroine of Atwood's short story, 'Under Glass'. She too wants desperately not to feel, to abdicate her humanity and become a plant, insensitive. She suffers in a destructive relationship with a man as insane as she; she dreams of giving birth to babies who are creatures from other planets, who are covered with fur, or who are born dead, 'scrawny as kittens' (*Dancing Girls*, 77). She haunts the zoo, but finds little comfort in the otters eating bones and detached heads, the tortoises in their cement cubicles, the echidnas, 'waddling through the sawdust like fat fur-coated madwomen' (85). Finally she prefers the greenhouse, the plants grown 'under glass', and particularly those plants which 'have taught themselves to look like stones. I think of them; they grow silently, hiding in dry soil, minor events, little zeros. . . . I wonder how long it takes, how they do it' (87).

What or who has 'killed' Atwood's protagonists and turned them into zeros, negatives? Perhaps, as the protagonist of *Surfacing* tells herself, it is an accident of some kind:

Woman sawn apart in a wooden crate, wearing a
bathing suit, smiling, a trick done with mirrors, I
read it in a comic book; only with me there had been
an accident and I came apart. The other half, the
one locked away, was the only one that could live; I
was the wrong half, detached, terminal. I was
nothing but a head, or, no, something minor like a
severed thumb; numb. (129)

Similar images of amputation, symbolising the
protagonist's own split psyche, occur on almost every page:
Madame in the grocery store who has one arm, the
protagonist and her brother wrapping their legs in blankets
and pretending 'the Germans shot our feet off' (9), the
schoolyard game of placing one's finger through a hole in a
box and pretending it was a 'dead finger', heads
metaphorically and literally separated from bodies. But
these are the projections of the protagonist's own psyche
just as surely as Marian in *The Edible Woman* chooses to
see and to create her world as imbued with images of
mouths and food. If the protagonist of *Surfacing* is dead, it
is because she has killed herself; if she is divided and
amputated, it is because she has chosen to see herself in
this way. There is a great deal of the existentialist in
Atwood: the world indeed is absurd, but what one chooses
to do about given conditions is one's own responsibility.
To decide not to decide, to remain in 'border country', is
in itself a decision. One is condemned to one's freedom
and must bear the responsibility for both action or refusal
to act. As Atwood has characterised her heroine in an
interview:

If you define yourself as intrinsically innocent, then
you have a lot of problems, because in fact you
aren't. And the thing with her is she wishes not to be
human. She wishes to be not human, because being

human inevitably involves being guilty, and if you define yourself as innocent, you can't accept that.[2]

In *Survival*, Atwood groups the subjects of Canadian literature into 'basic victim positions', and asks the central question, 'Who is responsible?' (*Survival*, 222). The answer to that question, provided in all of Atwood's books, is that responsibility lies almost inevitably in the self.

As the protagonist of *Surfacing* has divided herself, so she divides her world, projecting 'the good and the bad kind of everything' (44). Women are good and men are bad; little girls draw Easter bunnies and little boys draw torture scenes; women are innocent and men are rapists and exploiters in sexual relationships. The sexes are divided and isolated from each other much as in the little wooden barometer which impressed the protagonist as a child: the woman emerges from the little house on sunny days and the man on rainy days. So David and Anna, as the protagonist sees them, are divided and separated, he the criminal and she the victim, balanced forever in some terrible polarity of opposition, she hiding behind her make-up and the screen from her cigarette smoke, reading murder mysteries but never realising that she herself is the victim of another kind of murder. As the protagonist overhears Anna and David making love in the next room, she thinks of Anna's cry as that of 'an animal's at the moment the trap closes' (99). The protagonist cannot say to Joe that she loves him because that would be a capitulation, and he would be the victor, waving a flag, a 'parade' in his head.

As men destroy women in the protagonist's Manichean vision of the world, so groups and nations destroy and oppress other groups and nations. The military images associated with individual men have their prototype in Hitler, that bogey of the protagonist's childhood: '. . . when we were small the origin was Hitler, he was the great evil, many-tentacled, ancient and indestructible as the Devil' (153). But even when Hitler has been reduced in actuality to 'a few cinders and teeth', his evil manifests itself, like a tapeworm dividing, in 'the Americans', those oppressors of Canada and invaders of the wilderness. And still as an adult, the protagonist divides people into Canadians (victims) and Americans (victors). On the first page of the novel, the protagonist notes the pollution and the dying elm trees of her homeland caused by 'the disease spreading up from the south' (9). The Americans invade as hunters, as spoilers; 'Getting any?' they ask, referring to fish but alluding as well to sexual conquest. It is they, she thinks, who have killed the symbolic heron she discovers on the island, killed it for sport, mutilated and then crucified it, left it hanging in a tree 'like something in a butcher's window, desecrated, unredeemed' (154).

The heron is a metaphor for the protagonist's victimised self, for Canada as a nation, and for Christ as well. Animals, she feels, share the innocence of women and of Christian martyrs. All are dismembered, divided, rendered holy: 'miraculous in an unspecified way like the toes of saints or the cut-off pieces of early martyrs, the eyes on the plate, the severed breasts, the heart with letters on it shining like a light bulb through the trim hole painted in the chest, art history' (31). Like Marian in *The Edible Woman*, the protagonist finds it difficult to eat animals, rationalising her guilt for this act in a variety of ways: that the fish 'had chosen to die and forgiven me in advance' (72). The heron and all other animals killed for food become deified: '. . . anything that suffers and dies instead of us is Christ. . . . The animals die that we may live, they are substitute people, hunters in the fall killing the deer, that is Christ also. And we eat them, out of cans or otherwise; we are eaters of death, dead Christ-flesh resurrecting inside us, granting us life. Canned Spam, canned Jesus . . .' (164–65). Atwood's poem, 'Brian the

Still-Hunter', echoes a similar guilt: 'I kill because I have to/but every time I aim, I feel/my skin grow fur' (*The Journals of Susanna Moodie*, 36).

Even in childhood, the protagonist of *Surfacing* was fascinated with the idea of martyrdom and with religion, a subject as forbidden in her home as sex is in other homes. At school she exchanged information about sex for information about religion, although she was terrified by her idea that 'there was a dead man in the sky watching everything I did' (52). Just as self-destructive and illusory as Christianity in this context is the protagonist's sudden conversion, inspired by her father's diagrams of the cave paintings, to the ancient Indian religions. This crisis point occurs in the context of her discovery of her father's body. She is only now beginning to face the reality of her recent past and the abortion; she has possibly conceived a baby with Joe, and she has committed her one act of heroism in the destruction of 'Random Samples'. She escapes her friends, who now seem to her totally malevolent, and hides in the words where she reverts almost completely to an animal identity, wearing only a blanket which must serve her 'until the fur grows' (208). She imagines that she is now directed by a mysterious 'power', not that of 'the bland oleo-tinted Jesus prints . . . holy triple name shrunken to swear-words' (170), but of the Indian gods who had 'marked the sacred places, the places where you could learn the truth' (171). According to the dictates of the gods, she must avoid 'man-made' structures and objects; she must become a part of nature, immerse herself in it and discard her human form. She eats only the food of the gods, including an hallucinogenic mushroom, and a series of visions ensues. She loses herself in both place and time, becoming a part of the forest in its prehistoric state: 'The forest leaps upward, enormous, the way it was before they cut it, columns of sunlight frozen; the boulders float, melt, everything is made of water. . . . The animals have no need for speech, why talk when you are a word . . . I lean against a tree, I am a tree leaning' (212). And soon after, even the animal identity is suspended: 'I am not an animal or a tree, I am the thing in which the trees and animals move and grow, I am a place' (213). Both of her parents appear to her in separate visions, her mother, hands outstretched feeding the blue jays as the protagonist remembers her in life, and her father who is transformed before her eyes into a manifestation of her own madness, 'the thing you meet when you've stayed out here too long alone' (218).

Critical evaluations of Atwood's intentions in these passages are varied, and perhaps Atwood herself invites such diversity through her use of ambiguity. Feminist myth critic Annis Pratt sees the protagonist's sojourn in the wilderness as an archetypal quest '. . . in which the hero plunges down through subconscious to unconscious materials and is empowered by absorbing the archetypal symbols available to her at the fountainhead of her personality and being'.[3] The appearance of the mother and the essentially female imagery which dominates the descriptions of nature lead Pratt to conclude that Atwood and other women writers have

> . . . dug the goddess out of our ruins and cleansed
> the debris from her face, casting aside the gynophobic
> masks hiding her power and her beneficence. In so
> doing, they have made of women's fiction a pathway
> to the authentic self, the roots of our selves before
> consciousness of self, and shown us the way to the
> healing waters of our innermost being.[4]

In *Archetypal Patterns in Women's Fiction*, Pratt sees the protagonist's religious conversion and mysticism in terms of a 'reconciliation of the spiritual to the physical'.[5] Carol Christ in *Diving Deep and Surfacing* also sees the protagonist's experience as validly religious, as 'a revelation from great powers' which results in the achievement of 'authentic selfhood and power'.[6] Other critics are more cynical: Marie-Françoise Guedon in '*Surfacing*: Amerindian Themes and Shamanism' sees Atwood's representation of the out of body experience as inspired by shamanic tradition, but views her treatment of the gods as purely symbolic: there is, she argues, no coherent systematising of Indian motifs in Atwood, no 'Indian perception of the world. "Indian" people inhabit only the mind of the heroine'.[7] Jerome H. Rosenberg warns that 'feminist' readers should beware of overly subjective interpretations: '. . . we must prevent our spirits from travelling too deeply on interior journeys, lest we become lost and confused . . .'.[8]

Certainly Atwood is employing a version of what Joseph Campbell in *Hero with a Thousand Faces* refers to as the 'monomyth', the archetypal descent and return of the religious hero. She is also consciously making reference to initiation rites, which also have their origin in ancient religions, and which incorporate such patterns as the temporary withdrawal from society, the removal of the old clothing, the eating of new food, the symbolic arrival into adulthood. The myths are there; they are artistically useful, but they do not perhaps represent an ethos for Atwood or what she sees as a model of religious belief. Like Joseph Conrad's Marlowe in *The Heart of Darkness* who also journeys into an 'interior' of multiple symbolic significance including the discovery of the self, Atwood's heroine is, finally, no religious hero, no archetypal law-giver, but instead a better, more complete human being.

Atwood's primary interest, then, is the psychological rather than the mystical or the religious. The protagonist is close to mental collapse in the beginning of the novel, and she must actually break down before she can break through, as I have argued in a previous book, *Madness and Sexual*

*Politics in the Feminist Novel*.[9] Her immersion in the wilderness as well as her religious ecstasies are metaphors for her journey through her own subconscious mind, that place in which she can discover her past and affirm her identity, much as in a process of psychoanalysis. The gods are a manifestation of insanity, not a cure, but her visions and delusions lead her towards a confrontation with reality, with responsibility. One travels *through* the 'green world' of myth and delusion and innocence, as Atwood indicates in *Procedures for Underground*:

> The country beneath the earth has a green sun
> and the rivers flow backwards;
> the trees and rocks are the same
> as they are here, but shifted.
> Those who live there are always hungry;
> from them you can learn
> wisdom and great power
> if you can descend and return safely.

However, Atwood warns at the end of the poem, 'be careful/never to eat their food' ('Procedures for Underground', 25). One must always 'return safely', must 'surface' into a real world of sanity.

The descent and return pattern in Atwood's novel is also associated symbolically with images of rebirth. If the protagonist is 'dead' at the beginning of the novel, she must somehow be reborn, not in a religious sense, but psychologically. In order to re-create herself, she must re-create her parents, remove them also from the world of lies and myths where in her madness she has placed them. Her present conception of her father as insane, lurking in the woods and manifesting himself as a kind of wolf in a ghostly apparition, is only slightly more sophisticated than the old games of hide and seek in which '. . . even when we knew what tree he had gone behind there was the fear that what would come out when you called would be someone else' (58). The protagonist in this context is like the young cousins in Atwood's poem 'Game After Supper': 'though we giggle, we are afraid./From the shadows around/the corner of the house/a tall man is coming to find us:/He will be an uncle,/if we are lucky' (*Procedures for Underground*, 7). The father in *Surfacing* is in reality no monster, no devil figure with 'antlers in the brain', no god capable of metamorphosis, no madman, and he undoubtedly never experiences the visions which the protagonist imagines for him, visions of 'stepping through a usual door and finding yourself in a different galaxy, purple trees and red moons and a green sun' (171). His reality is that of a reasonable person, a scientist, a believer in the mode of the eighteenth-century rationalists. He wanted to protect his children from the evils of a society torn by World War II and from the negative effects of superstitions like religion. His limitations are those of reason and logic, male attributes in the protagonist's mind, but he is also benevolent, both guide and map-maker.

While the ostensible search on the island is for the father, the metaphoric search is for the mother. The protagonist, like other of Atwood's fictional and poetic heroines, is a kind of Persephone who must return from the underworld to find and to re-create herself in her mother. And the protagonist insists for a time that her mother is, in fact, a Demeter, a goddess capable of restoring life to the dead as she revives the protagonist's brother from near death by drowning. It is somehow a betrayal that the mother refuses to resurrect herself from death, to 'get out of that glass case' like Snow White, and 'go away by herself into the forest' (176). The protagonist believes that her mother possessed a kind of magic, an ability to charm the animals, conjure the blue jays and command a bear. Her power is perceived as extending to include all of nature itself, as she records and thus orders the seasons and the weather in her magic journal. Wearing her powerful leather jacket and her hair in a style of 'thirty years ago', she is capable of transcending time: 'Impossible to be like my mother', the protagonist believes, 'it would need a time warp; she was either ten thousand years behind the rest or fifty years ahead of them' (60).

But the protagonist must indeed become like her mother. In order to be reborn, to heal her divided psyche, she must receive a 'legacy' from both parents; she has received the gift of knowledge from her father, but her mother's gift, yet to be discovered, will be 'beyond logic'. She is mysteriously guided, she believes, to one of her own childhood drawings, a picture of a woman 'with a round moon stomach: the baby was sitting up inside gazing out' (185), just as the protagonist has earlier envisioned herself as conscious before her birth, able to see the world through her mother's transparent womb. She interprets the picture as an instruction: to become alive, she must resurrect that part of herself which she has killed; she must replace her aborted baby and become, like her mother in the picture, 'the miraculous double woman' giving birth to herself as well as to new life. The protagonist takes her lover to the shore of the lake and carefully arranges their positions:

> I lie down, keeping the moon on my left hand and the absent sun on my right. He kneels . . . . He trembles and then I can feel my lost child surfacing within me, forgiving me, rising from the lake where it has been prisoned for so long, its eyes and teeth phosphorescent; the two halves clasp, interlocking like fingers, it buds, it sends out fronds. . . . it will be covered with shining fur, a god, I will never teach it any words. (190–191)

From this point onward, the novel replaces the images of division and death with images of unity, wholeness, life.

However, Atwood is again ambiguous: even the ritual conception is a re-enactment of the childhood drawings of 'heaven', the moon and the sun in perfect balance. Also her belief that she is to be forgiven by her aborted baby, who fish-like 'drowned in air', is reminiscent of her childish conviction that the fish she eats 'forgive her in advance'. Still suffering from delusions of her own innocence, the protagonist has yet to enter and confront her own madness.

Only after her withdrawal into the forest where 'there are no longer any rational points of view' (199), where she loses her identity, worships the Indian gods which she confuses with her parents, and experiences visions, can the protagonist truly be reborn into the adult she must become in order to survive. One of the first indications that she is, perhaps for the first time, truly human, is that she restores her parents to *their* humanity, removes them from 'behind a wall as translucent as Jell-O, mammoths frozen in a glacier' (11), from the Edenic state of innocence where she has placed them. She is like the speaker in the poem 'Eden is a Zoo' who keeps her 'parents in a garden/among lumpy trees, green sponges/on popsicle sticks' (*Procedures for Underground*, 6). The protagonist of *Surfacing* allows her parents, finally, to go 'back into the earth, the air, the water, wherever they were when I summoned them' (219). 'To prefer life, I owe them that' (220), she affirms, and her sanity is finally secure with her existential recognition that there is, in fact,

> No total salvation, resurrection, Our father, Our mother, I pray, Reach down for me, but it won't work: they dwindle, grow, become what they were, human. Something I never gave them credit for; but their totalitarian innocence was my own. (221)

The gods also become what they were, projections of the protagonist's own madness: 'No gods to help me now, they're questionable once more, theoretical as Jesus'. They will not appear to her again, because 'I can't afford it; from now on I'll have to live in the usual way, defining them by their absence . . . they give only one kind of truth' (221). Even the baby, 'perhaps not real, even that is uncertain', is restored to human status: 'No god . . . it might be the first one, the first true human' (223). Nature itself, formerly an extension of the gods, also becomes real, understandable, benign: 'the lake is quiet, the trees surround me, asking and giving nothing' (224).

The ultimate affirmation of sanity and humanity, however, is provided by the symbolic mirror, that agent of truth and objective reality in which the protagonist asserts her identity and rejects her madness: 'I turn the mirror around: in it there's a creature neither animal nor human, furless . . . eyes staring blue as ice from the deep sockets. . . . This was the stereotype, straws in the hair, talking nonsense or not talking at all' (222). Language again becomes meaningful; it is human to communicate: 'For us it is necessary, the intercession of words' (224). The protagonist's perception of her world has changed; divisions and polarities exist, but they can be dealt with, even 'the Americans', who are advancing, 'can be watched and predicted and stopped' (221). Most important, the protagonist is no longer seeing herself as victim, but as human and responsible:

> This above all, to refuse to be a victim. Unless I can do that I can do nothing. I have to recant, give up the old belief that I am powerless and because of it nothing I can do will ever hurt anyone. A lie which was always more disastrous than the truth would have been. (222–223)

She is ready to rejoin society. Joe calls her name and waits, 'a mediator, an ambassador' (224). 'To immerse oneself, join in the war, or to be destroyed. Though there ought to be other choices' (220), she says, realising that she is now capable of commitment, action: 'withdrawing is no longer possible and the alternative is death' (223). The protagonist's world is not perfect, not 'heaven', but neither is it the hell of madness: she is out of 'border country'.

*The Journals of Susanna Moodie* was written slightly earlier than *Surfacing*, and the historical pioneer protagonist of the poems bears a considerable resemblance to her modern counterpart, who is also a kind of pioneer in that wilderness which is the modern world, a tourist in a foreign country. Susanna Moodie also lives in 'border country', a stranger in her own world, divided and half insane, torn between love and hate for the wilderness in which she finds herself immersed. Like the protagonist of *Surfacing*, Susanna Moodie has lost herself; she refuses to look in mirrors, even 'The moving water will not show me/my reflection' (*The Journals of Susanna Moodie*, 11). When finally, after years of living in the wilderness, she does confront herself, she sees a vision much like that of the reflected protagonist in *Surfacing*: her 'skin thickened/with bark and the white hairs of roots' (24). Susanna Moodie, too, is doubled and divided, perceiving her world as dominated by terrible polarities. In 'The Double Voice', Susanna Moodie recognises that 'Two voices/took turns using my eyes'. The first voice praises the beauty of Canada, extolling the virtues of mountains and rivers; the other confronts a 'dead dog/jubilant with maggots/half-buried among the sweet peas' (42). She dreams of her bush garden where she picks strawberries, but in the dream, the strawberries stain her hands: 'I should have known/anything planted here/would come up blood' (34).

As the protagonist of *Surfacing* meets adversity by symbolically transforming herself into an animal, so Susanna Moodie conceives of herself in grotesque animal images: her brain 'gropes nervous/tentacles', her fears are 'hairy as bears', she needs 'wolf's eyes to see/the truth' (13), on her aging face 'the wrinkles branch/out, overlapping like hair or feathers', and at her death, she thinks, she will 'prowl and slink/in crystal darkness . . . with new/formed plumage . . ./my fingers/curving and scaled' (49). 'In time the animals/arrived to inhabit me' (26), she says, while at other times she imagines herself as a plant, her fingers 'brittle as twigs', her eyes 'blind/buds, which can see/only the wind' (25); 'at the last/judgement we will all be trees' (59). She transforms others as well as herself: her husband walks into the forest in 'The Wereman'; as he disappears from sight, she asks 'what does he change into/what other shape/blends with the under-/growth' (19).

Mrs Moodie's transformations are credited to art, magic, witchcraft. She is a version of the Hecate figure of the Triple Goddess which Atwood defines in *Survival*, solely responsible for the creation of her world, a fact she understands much more clearly than does the protagonist of *Surfacing*. She knows that in the wilderness or in the mind, aspects of a single entity, 'you find only/the shape you already are' (25). But also like the protagonist of *Surfacing*, Susanna Moodie is a 'failed artist', a writer frustrated by her own inability to define herself as artist. Her 'disintegrated children' are emblematic of this failure, and they clutch at her skirts with their dead fingers, like briars, like guilt (41).

Unlike *Surfacing*, there can be no resolution of sanity and completion in *The Journals of Susanna Moodie*. The speaker in the poems remains divided, herself symbolic of the 'violent duality' with which Atwood characterises Canada (62). The best that can be construed is that she ultimately 'accepts the reality of the country she is in, and . . . she accepts also the inescapable doubleness of her own vision', as Atwood explains in the Afterword (63). In the last poem, 'A Bus Along St. Clair: December', Susanna

Moodie has transcended her death and, witch-like, has
returned to curse the very civilisation she once longed for:
'I am the old woman/sitting across from you on the bus',
she warns, and, 'out of her eyes come secret/hatpins,
destroying/the walls, the ceiling'. She transforms the city
back into the wilderness: 'there is no city;/this is a
forest/your place is empty' (61).

*The Journals of Susanna Moodie* is the most narrative in
style and structure of Atwood's poems, just as *Surfacing* is
the most poetic of her novels. These two major works
share a wealth of similar images; both are maps to the
psyches of individual heroines, yet also to some vaster
concept of the Canadian mind. 'My mind is a wide pink
map', says Susanna Moodie, 'across which move year after
year/arrows and dotted lines' (33). In the Afterword to the
poems, Atwood compares Susanna Moodie's doubleness to
the 'paranoid schizophrenia' that is Canada. As Sherill E.
Grace writes in 'Margaret Atwood and the Poetics of
Duplicity', the *Journals* are 'at once an emblem of Canada's
cultural past, a model for national potential and a symbol
of human physiological, psychological, and linguistic
doubleness'.[10]

The same might be said of *Surfacing*, which, like the
*Journals*, could not have been written about any other
country in the world. Susanna Moodie is, in fact, the
landscape, the female tradition, through which the
protagonist of *Surfacing* searches for her identity. Identity,
for Atwood, is always to be discovered through a recognition
of one's relationship to one's ancestors. As Atwood also
establishes in 'Five Poems for Grandmothers', 'one woman
leads to another./Finally I know you/through your
daughters,/my mother, her sisters,/and through myself'
(*Two-Headed Poems*, 38). Identity and sanity, at least for
the protagonist of *Surfacing*, ultimately lie in the
confrontation with the outer duality of Canada reflected in
the inner duality of the self. One sees the self in the context

of a national history, and faces the paradox that 'history/breeds death', but 'if you kill/it you will kill yourself' (*Two-Headed Poems*, 71).

# 4 The 'Escape Artist': *Lady Oracle*

In a poem entitled 'Hesitations outside the Door', Atwood writes, 'If we make stories for each other/about what is in the room/we will never have to go in . . .' (*Selected Poems*, 171). She refers to the story of Bluebeard and the forbidden castle room which contains the bodies of murdered former wives, 'the thin women' who hang 'on their hooks, dismembered'. But Atwood is also making a statement about the misuse of art; she implies that one may escape confrontation with reality by creating fiction. As the protagonist of *Surfacing* misuses art to create an alternative and more ideal world through her drawings and her 'alibis', so Joan Foster of *Lady Oracle* is also an 'escape artist' (367), intent on evading reality and commitment by 'writing' her world. She moves through mirrors and through her own self-deluding fictions into a realm of fairy tales and myth where, instead of escaping, she becomes trapped in the very surfaces she strives to create. Although she searches for her self in many mirrors and in the numerous gothic romances she writes for her living, romances in which all the heroines are always versions of herself, Joan never comes to terms with a reality beneath the surface of her schizophrenic existence. Like Cervantes' Don Quixote or Henry James's Isabel Archer or Flaubert's

Emma Bovary or any number of other literary heroes and heroines who substitute art for life and fictive roles for their own identities, Joan models her life after a concept of romance: 'All my life,' she says, 'I'd been hooked on plots' (342).

The first 'plots' one encounters in childhood are, of course, fairy tales, and Joan conceives of even her adult life as a series of recognisable patterns. Quite early in the novel, she adopts the role of Snow White, that image of virtue and victimisation who is the object of the wrath and envy of the evil stepmother. Joan's actual mother, whom Joan often imagines to be her stepmother, is preoccupied with beauty. Like the evil queen, she sits before her magic mirror in Joan's childhood memory and in her recurring dream; Joan is permitted to watch while her mother applies her make-up and her 'double mouth' (71), the mouth of lipstick over the shadow of her real lips:

> I would stare at the proceedings, fascinated and
> mute. I thought my mother was very beautiful, even
> more beautiful when she was colored in. And this
> was what I did in the dream: I sat and stared . . .
> my mother always had a triple mirror, so she could
> see both sides as well as the front of her head. In the
> dream, as I watched, I suddenly realised that instead
> of three reflections she had three actual heads, which
> rose from her toweled shoulders on three separate
> necks. This didn't frighten me, as it seemed merely
> a confirmation of something I'd always known: . . .
> my mother was a monster. (70)

Joan's mother does indeed have a 'double mouth' which says one thing and means another. She wears white gloves which disguise her blood-red nails in Joan's vision of her; she never touches or kisses. Her temper is violent and, in fact, she precipitates Joan's flight from home by actually stabbing her daughter with a kitchen knife. But it is the queen and not Snow White who, in this story, is prematurely entombed in the glass coffin which is her suburban house, a 'plastic-shrouded tomb from which there was no exit' (201). Her punishment will be an early death, not from dancing in red-hot iron shoes as actually happens in the Snow White story and symbolically in so many of Atwood's 'dancing girl' stories, but from tripping over her floppy pink bedroom slippers and falling down the basement stairs.

Joan's mother is a Walt Disney version of evil, an anomaly in Atwood's complex fictional world in which characters are seldom so simplistic. It is, then, altogether possible that she represents, at least partly, Joan's subjective projection. Joan sees her as a single entity, a monster, but the mirror, as is usually the case in Atwood's fiction and poetry, reflects the true and multiple image. Joan is our only narrator, and she is almost as unreliable as the narrator of *Surfacing*. By her own admission a 'compulsive and romantic' liar (165), she is telling the story, which is this novel, to a reporter, a man in whom she is interested and to whom she 'didn't tell any lies. Well, not many . . . but nothing major' (378). Along with all her other fabrications, Joan perhaps creates this image of her mother as the evil queen in order to preserve her corresponding image of herself as Snow White. The myth is necessary to her, and, as she tells the reporter, she cannot bear to part with her fantasy mother, with 'the image of her that I carried for years, hanging from my neck like an iron locket' (71).

Joan periodically conjures her mother's ghost, imagining that she is being visited by an 'astral body', one wearing a navy suit and neat white gloves, mascara streaming down the cheeks in black tears. Joan does ultimately come to a sort of recognition, a final confrontation with her mother's ghost in which she realises that 'She'd never really let go of me because I had never let her go. It had been she standing behind me in the mirror. . . . My mother was a vortex, a dark vacuum, I would never be able to make her happy. . . . Maybe it was time for me to stop trying' (363). But Joan does not ever truly recognise her complicity in this relationship with the evil stepmother who is her double, a reflected version of herself, nor does she ever successfully extricate herself from the vortex which is her own inability to confront this and other realities.

Many of Joan's mythologically-inspired identities, like the Snow White persona, are derived from mirrors; even the fat lady image is one she sees reflected in a fun-house mirror as a child. As Marian in *The Edible Woman* rejects her female identity, her 'role as Woman', by refusing to eat, so Joan rejects her prescribed roles by eating to excess until the real Joan is hidden and protected in a cocoon of fat, a 'magic cloak of blubber and invisibility' (157). Thus she successfully evades the sexual attentions of men, while, at the same time, she manages to enrage her mother: 'I had defeated her: I wouldn't ever let her make me over in her image, thin and beautiful' (94). To be 'thin and beautiful', according to the psychiatrist to whom Joan is sent by her mother, is the prerequisite for marriage, and given the disaster which is her parents' marriage, Joan prefers exemption. Like the protagonist of *Surfacing*, she simply 'refuses to play'. 'But why did I feel I had to be excused', Joan asks. 'Why did I want to be exempted, and what from? In high school you didn't have to play baseball if you had your period or a pain in your stomach, and I preferred the sidelines' (242).

For the rest of the novel, Joan's recurring vision is of the fat lady self, not on the sidelines, but in the spotlight, dressed in an obscene tutu, dancing on a highwire. This particular fiction is inspired by her childhood experience in which her mother and her dancing teacher in collusion decide that Joan is too plump to make a convincing butterfly in the ballet recital. She is accordingly robbed of her wings and reduced to the role of moth ball. Even years later when Joan sheds her pounds of fat, emerging finally into the role of butterfly, she is haunted by the ghost of her fat self, 'my dark twin. . . . She wanted to kill me and take my place' (279).

The fat lady in the tutu, who works in the same 'freak show' with the 'dancing girls', also has a double, another of Atwood's 'dancing girls' who recur throughout the poetry and fiction in any variety of disguises. Moira Shearer in *The Red Shoes* (whose importance as an image for Atwood is discussed in Chapter 1) also becomes an identity for Joan, who shares the luxurious red hair of her idol and who repeatedly attempts to also dance herself to death and to suffer 'more than anyone' (87). Joan is still Moira Shearer at the end of the novel when, her entire life in a shambles, she decides to 'dance for no one but myself':

> I raised myself onto my bare toes and twirled around,
> tentatively at first. The air filled with spangles. I
> lifted my arms and swayed them in time to the gentle
> music, I remembered the music, I remembered
> every step and gesture. . . . I closed my eyes. Wings
> grew from my shoulders. . . . I'd danced right
> through the broken glass, in my bare feet too. Some
> butterfly . . . . The real red shoes, the feet punished
> for dancing. You could dance, or you could have the
> love of a good man. But you were afraid to dance,
> because you had this unnatural fear that if you
> danced they'd cut your feet off so you wouldn't be
> able to dance. Finally you overcame your fear and
> danced, and they cut your feet off. The good man
> went away too, because you wanted to dance (368).

Both Moira Shearer and the fat lady then merge identities with that other innocent and victimised heroine, yet another 'dancing girl' identity for Joan, the Little Mermaid of the fairy tale who traded her tongue for legs only to find herself dancing at the prince's wedding to somebody else. Again, Atwood invokes her familiar paradox of the woman as artist: to sacrifice art for love is to sacrifice art, love and the self as well.

Still another of Joan's identities is also a victim of the same paradox. The Lady of Shalott sits in her gothic tower weaving her ornate tapestries, creating her art and watching the medieval world through a mirror. She is content until the reflection of the handsome knight appears, at which point she leaves the tower, the tapestry, and the mirror in search of love, only to encounter her own death and minimal attention from the knight who barely notices as she floats by in her death barge. Joan has the Tennyson poem in mind, but perhaps Atwood also identifies her with the Pre-Raphaelite painting by William Holman Hunt of the Lady of Shalott. An ornate mirror dominates the painting, and the central figure of a woman is a caricature of femininity with her baroque and wild red hair (the colour of Joan's). She wears the costume of a dancing girl, and she appears to be entangled in the threads from her own weaving. Like Homer's Penelope or any number of other weaving or spinning women in mythology and literature (including Philomela, who, like the Little Mermaid, also lost her tongue), the lady in Holman Hunt's painting represents a fearful kind of witch-like power. The hair, like the weaving, symbolises power of a sexual nature; it can function to ensnare men, as is also true in the case of Rapunzel (whom Atwood sees in *Survival* as a prototype for Canadian literary heroines), or Circe (another of Atwood's woman/artist heroines in 'Circe/Mud Poems'), or even snake-haired Medusa, the original 'girl with the Gorgon touch' (whose image dominates in *Double Persephone*). All of these ultimately doomed women of mythology, regardless of how powerful they may be in the beginning, end in sorry circumstances, and thus they represent a warning: untold dangers await the woman who presumes to see herself as artist.

Joan, too, perceives herself as doomed to a tragic fate; her life, she thinks, is out of her control. On the first page of the novel, she invokes the dual images of the fat lady and the Lady of Shalott as metaphors for her own life, which, she says, 'had a tendency to spread, to get flabby, to scroll and festoon like the frame of a baroque mirror' (3). Isolated in a metaphoric tower which she only partly realises is of her own creation, Joan plays her part of the artist, writing her gothic novels and gazing in a mirror at her concept of reality. The 'knight' she invents for her medieval lady self is her husband, appropriately named Arthur. Finally, Joan choreographs her own 'death' to correspond to Tennyson's poem (and perhaps to another Pre-Raphaelite painting, that by John William Waterhouse which depicts the Lady of Shalott floating in a barge down a beautiful river, her long red hair as remarkable here as in Holman Hunt's painting). Joan becomes 'the lady in the boat, the death barge, the tragic lady with flowing hair and stricken eyes, the lady in the tower. She couldn't stand the view from the window, life was her curse' (363). Joan too cannot stand the view of her own life, and, attempting to untangle herself from her ornate tapestry of lies, she imitates her own suicide, pretending to have drowned but actually floating to the illusion of freedom in a death barge. Unlike the 'drownings' in Atwood's poems and in *Surfacing*, this journey under water is not revelatory, but rather part of the con-game which is Joan's life. She holds on to her fictions: 'You could stay in the tower for years', she says, 'weaving away, looking in the mirror, but one glance out the window at real life and that was that. The curse, the doom' (346).

Joan's early fascination with her mother's kind of art practised ritualistically before the three-way mirror is never dispelled; significantly, the adult Joan also buys herself a triple mirror in front of which she, too, perpetrates an illusion. It is here that her real literary career as Lady Oracle begins. Acting on the advice of spiritualist Leda Sprott, Joan begins her experiments with automatic writing, another indication of a failure to accept responsibility for her actions. She lights a candle, seats herself at the mirror, closes her eyes and enters a 'dark, shining corridor' (246). When she returns, she finds a series of words manifested on the paper before her; predictably, these evolve into a poem which relies heavily on imagery involving the Lady of Shalott 'standing in the prow' of 'the death boat', singing and crying simultaneously. The lady of Joan's poem lives 'under the earth somewhere, or inside something, a cave or a huge building'; she is 'enormously powerful, like a goddess, but it was an unhappy power' (248). Ultimately, Joan's creation evolves into 'the redgold lady' who has lost her 'glass wings' (252), and she is thus related to the rest of Joan's heroines, all of whom are, of course, herself.

The goddess identity also persists throughout Joan's fantasies. Her first lover, Paul, has said to Joan's thin self that she has 'the body of a goddess' (158). But Joan has seen depictions of headless and armless Venuses, mutilated women like the wives of Bluebeard, and she rejects the analogy. Some years later, Joan visits the Tivoli in Italy with Arthur where she encounters the fountain statue of Diana of Ephesus, a kind of fertility goddess whose 'serene face' is 'perched on top of a body shaped like a mound of grapes. She was draped in breasts from neck to ankle, as though afflicted with a case of yaws. . . . The nipples were equipped with spouts, but several of the breasts were out of order'. Joan rejects this fantasy of the goddess as fat lady and as archetypal mother as well: 'Once I would have seen her as an image of myself, but not any more. My ability to give was limited, I was not inexhaustible' (282).

Joan's triple mirror not only inspires her Lady Oracle

poems, but her later gothic novels as well. These she
writes with her eyes closed, refusing to take the
consequences for what she commits to paper: 'It was
somehow inhibiting to have to see what I'd put on the
page' (146). When Joan sits at the mirror and closes the
two sides around her, her own image becomes multiplied
to an infinite number, 'extending in a line as far as I could
see' (245). She is also thus able to create the illusion of a
mirror maze, a correspondingly infinite number of doors
and hallways, like the sinister maze in her current novel,
*Stalked by Love*, which confuses and entraps Felicia, the
red-haired wife who takes over the novel in spite of Joan
and Charlotte, the appropriate 'good' heroine. What Felicia
and Joan both discover in the 'central plot' of the maze is
multiple manifestations of themselves; they themselves are
all the wives of Bluebeard, all the mythological victims and
'dancing girls' of fairy-tale tradition:

> Suddenly she found herself in the central plot. A
> stone bench ran along one side, and on it were
> seated four women. Two of them looked a lot like
> her, with red hair and green eyes and small white
> teeth. The third was middle-aged, dressed in a
> strange garment that ended halfway up her calves,
> with ratty piece of fur around her neck. The last
> was enormously fat. She was wearing a pair of pink
> tights and a short pink skirt covered with spangles.
> From her head sprouted two antennae, like a
> butterfly's, and a pair of obviously false wings was
> pinned to her back . . . 'We are Lady Redmond'
> . . . . (375–76)

There is no exit from this maze, nor from the multiplicity
of Joan's identities. Just as Joan has been trapped in the
mirror maze at an earlier point, '. . . stuck there, in the
midst of darkness, unable to move' (249), so she is caught

up in her own fictions, entangled, like Holman Hunt's Lady of Shalott, in the threads of her own art.

As in Atwood's earlier novels, the mirror as a symbol for art represents a basic and inescapable paradox: it is simultaneously a trap and an instrument of truth. As Atwood's earlier heroines, like Alice in Wonderland or Persephone in the underworld, must symbolically journey underground in order to discover truth and identity, so Joan must enter the mirror maze to find her many selves. Atwood has remarked in an interview that the maze in *Lady Oracle* is 'a descent into the underworld. There's a passage in Virgil's *Aeneid* which I found very useful, where Aeneas goes to the underworld to learn about his future. He's guided by the Sibyl and he learns what he has to from his dead father, and then he returns home'.[1] While the heroine of *Surfacing* emerges with knowledge from the 'tangled maze' of the island wilderness, Joan never seems to learn from the maze 'what she has to': that there is no escape from the confrontation with doubleness, multiplicity. Art, like the mirror, is ambiguous and dangerous, lending itself readily to misuse by the creation of lies, but leading finally to an inevitable confrontation with reality. Joan longs to enter the long dark corridor in the mirror where she imagines she might find '. . . the thing, the truth or word or person that was mine, that was waiting for me' (247), but there is no single or integrated person for her to find. Neither Snow White nor Joan ever truly learns what the evil stepmother always knew: that magic mirrors are condemned to the truth, and truth is inevitably and inescapably multiple and complex.

In *Lady Oracle*, as in all of her novels, Atwood explores identities through the symbolism of names. Joan's names, like her personality, are multiple and reflective of the fantasy world from which they are most often derived. She was named for film-star Joan Crawford, a pseudonym for the actual Lucille Le Seur. Her maiden name is Joan

Delacourt, her married name is Foster, her pen name is
Louisa K. Delacourt (after her aunt), and she is also Lady
Oracle. With each name, Joan is 're-born' into a new
personality, all of which are variations on her own theme.
She describes her emergence from the cocoon of fat as a
rebirth into a new self; marrying Arthur is an assumption
of a new personality; beginning an affair with 'the Royal
Porcupine' leads her to the realisation that 'This was the
beginning of my double life' (274); and the faked death by
drowning leads to a new identity in Italy. Even cutting and
dying her hair, Joan believes, will provide a new life and
an escape from the problems which so beset the old Joan.
'I was more than double', Joan says, 'I was triple, multiple,
and now I could see that there was more than one life to
come, there were many' (274).

Joan's numerous names and personalities lead Jerome
Rosenberg in *Margaret Atwood* to conclude that Atwood is
portraying '. . . something like multiple personality
disorder, in which traumatic episodes initiated in early
childhood trigger the formation of separate personalities
which constitute distinct parts of the victim's psyche and
exist side by side'.[2] However, Joan is not idiosyncratic in
her disorder, which, Atwood implies, might be symptomatic
of the female condition: '. . . men who changed their
names were likely to be conmen, criminals, undercover
agents or magicians, whereas women who changed their
names were probably just married' (226). Joan's protean
nature is reflected in the other women who populate her
actual as well as her fictional world. They are female
magicians, capable of transforming themselves from fairy
godmother to evil queen and back again.

Aunt Lou, for example, is perceived as the good mother,
loving, permissive, and cuddly:

> Aunt Lou . . . was soft, billowy, woolly, befurred;
> even her face, powdered and rouged, was covered

with tiny hairs, like a bee. Wisps escaped from her
head, threads from her hems, sweetish odors from
the space between her collar and her neck, where I
would rest my forehead, listening to the stories of
her talking fox. (95–96)

Through the medium of her talking fox stole, Aunt Lou
opens the world of fantasy, of stories, of romantic movies
like *The Red Shoes*, of carnivals and spiritualist gatherings.
It is she who waves her magic wand and originates those
fictions which Joan never outgrows. It is not surprising
that Joan borrows Aunt Lou's very name in her career as
gothic novelist. Aunt Lou's own literary career consists of
signing her name to pamphlets on menstruation, pamphlets
which perpetrate the outrageous lie that 'Growing up can
be fun' (91). Like Aunt Lou, Joan also lies to her readers
as well as to herself. She too provides fantasy and escape
for the women who buy her books in drugstores, 'neatly
packaged like the other painkillers' (34).

Aunt Lou, in fact, is a walking paradox. Playing the role
of maiden aunt, she conceals from Joan for years the fact
that she was once married and now has a married lover.
Fat herself, Aunt Lou understands the psychology of
obesity, yet she abets Joan in her fat lady disguise by
treating her to ice cream, crab meat sandwiches and gallons
of popcorn. She then confounds the ambiguity by leaving a
will resembling the archetypal bargain of fairy tales: Joan
must lose one hundred pounds before she can inherit her
legacy, the money that will free her from her mother and
allow her to begin a new life. Thus, Aunt Lou's mixed
messages add to Joan's confusion; the fairy godmother
changes Cinderella into the princess, and then introduces
her to Bluebeard. Although her mother seems always to
have been the stage director of Joan's life, Aunt Lou and
Joan herself have been in reality the secret choreographers
of destruction.

Aunt Lou also functions indirectly in the initiation of Joan's career as gothic novelist by introducing her to yet another enigmatic double lady, the spiritualist Leda Sprott. As proprietor of Jordan Chapel, Leda Sprott conducts seances, conjures Joan's mother who is not at this point dead, predicts the circumstances of Aunt Lou's death by heart failure after slipping on a bath mat, and promulgates the art of automatic writing. 'You have great gifts . . . great powers' (122), she tells Joan. Clearly, Leda Sprott is a perpetrator of lies, and yet Atwood permits her to redeem herself. Years later when Leda Sprott has become the Reverend Eunice P. Revele and performs Joan's marriage ceremony to Arthur, she is transformed into a kind of Sibyl, as in the Aeneas legend. She provides revelations, as her new name indicates is her function, and her advice to Joan is little short of oracular:

> You do not choose a gift, it chooses you, and if you deny it it will make use of you in any case, though perhaps in a less desirable way. I used my own gift, as long as I had it. You may think I'm a stupid old woman or a charlatan, I'm used to that. But sometimes I had the truth to tell: there's no mistaking it when you do. When I had no truth to tell, I told them what they wanted to hear. I shouldn't have done that. You may think it's harmless, but it isn't. . . . People have faith in you. . . . They trust you. That can be dangerous, especially if you take advantage of it. Everything catches up to you sooner or later. . . . Don't say what you don't mean. (229–230)

Leda Sprott alias Eunice P. Revele has one good eye and one bad eye. Like the rest of Atwood's literary characters, she is split, multiple, complex. But the truth she has to tell is one aspect of Atwood's own philosophy of literature and summarises what Atwood has stated in both poetry and fiction as the proper function of art.

Joan confuses life and art, truth and fiction. Her lover, the Royal Porcupine, inventor and sole practitioner of 'con-create art' (268), alias Chuck Brewer, commercial designer, is as schizophrenic as Joan, but in one sense, he does not misuse art in the same way that she does. Like Joe's squashed pots in *Surfacing*, the squashed and frozen animals displayed by the Royal Porcupine have a kind of bizarre integrity. On the one hand, these destroyed and mutilated animals, found along highways and preserved in a giant freezer, represent victims of civilisation; they manifest that fixation of the Canadian psyche with victimisation which Atwood discusses in *Survival*. Carefully preserved in the positions in which they were found, labelled as to place of discovery and actual cause of death, they also represent a form of truth, even, if one stretches the imagination, a political statement of an ecological nature. 'The new poetry', explains the Royal Porcupine, 'is the poetry of *things* (269). This is 'truth' taken to extremes, but at least the Royal Porcupine is generally sincere, which is a great deal more than can be said for Joan.

The aspect of truth which Joan continues to repress, even though it is manifested so obviously in her own mirror, in every person in her world, and is intrinsic in her own psyche, is that aspect of multiplicity. 'But every man has more than one wife', explain Joan's discarded selves at the centre of the maze in *Stalked by Love*, 'Sometimes all at once, sometimes one at a time, sometimes ones he doesn't even know about' (376). Arthur, for example, never solves the mystery of Joan's complexity; she never permits him to discover the gothic novelist beneath the surface of the inept housewife. Joan's fat lady identity also remains a secret, relegated to old photographs and identified to Arthur as 'Aunt Deirdre . . . Aunt Deirdre was a bitch' (98).

And it is also true that every woman has more than one husband, men being as doubled and multiplied as women in Atwood's books. Just as the multiple Joan is represented by the murdered wives of Redmond in *Stalked by Love*, so Redmond is a composite of all the men in Joan's life. Joan's father, whom she perceives as so ineffectual in comparison to her dominant mother, is ultimately revealed as a kind of Merlin who, in the practice of medicine, returns life to people whether they want it or not, and, in the practice of war, is responsible for the deaths of people who wanted life. In his role as anesthesiologist, he can simulate the deaths of living people. 'He was a man in a cage, like other men,' Joan observes, 'but what made him different was his dabbling in lives and deaths' (154). One of the faces of Redmond encountered at the centre of the maze is swathed in 'a white gauze mask' (377).

Joan is taught in childhood that there are 'two categories: nice men did things for you, bad men did things to you' (73). But she soon learns that life, and particularly men, defy classification. The 'daffodil man' might be the perverted exhibitionist whom little Joan encounters on her way home from a Brownie meeting (another version of Atwood's ubiquitous 'Underwear Man' from *The Edible Woman*), or he might be the rescuer who frees her from the tree to which her malicious sister Brownies have tied her. Even more disconcerting, perhaps he is both, just as Joan's Polish count in London is both Paul, the heroic political refugee, and Mavis Quilp, the author of *Lucy Gallant: Army Nurse*. The cloaked figure of the Royal Porcupine, eccentric artist and romantic lover, hides the identity of Chuck Brewer, '. . . gray and multidimensional and complicated like everyone else. Was every Heathcliff a Linton in disguise?' (300).

Arthur is perhaps less readily understandable than the other male characters Joan invents for the romance she sees as her life, but he, too, is multiple:

> Every man I'd ever been involved with, I realized,
> had had two selves: my father, healer and killer; the
> man in the tweed coat, my rescuer and possibly also
> a pervert; the Royal Porcupine and his double,
> Chuck Brewer; even Paul, who I'd always believed
> had a sinister other life I couldn't penetrate. Why
> should Arthur be any exception? . . . Arthur was
> someone I didn't know at all. And he was right in
> bed beside me . . . what if he woke up, eyes
> glittering, and reached for me . . . ? (325–326)

Hiding behind the mask of a 'Linton', an ineffectual idealist, a dispenser of socialist pamphlets, could be the mad Marxist, the potential bomber. Many identities in one, Arthur is by himself the peanut-crunching crowd gathered to watch Joan's show. She imagines herself at the centre of the Colosseum amidst '. . . noise and tumult, cheering crowds, death on the sands, wild animals growling, snarling, screams, and martyrs weeping in the wings . . .' (16). There Arthur sits, 'front row center . . . from time to time making a slight gesture that would preserve or destroy: thumbs up or thumbs down' (17).

The Colosseum fantasy is, of course, stolen from films, as are most of Joan's plots and characters, whether for her novels or for her life. Unlike Atwood, Joan is not a very literary kind of writer: she does not know who Tolstoy is, and she remembers 'The Lady of Shalott' only from her early school experience with *Narrative Poems for Juniors*. Her plots are via Walt Disney rather than the Brothers Grimm. Under Joan's scrutiny, the mythic fat woman of the Fellini films is reduced to Disney's *The Whale Who Wanted to Sing at the Met* (6). Her gothic romances are parodies of the genre, and even her Lady Oracle poems are 'a mixture of Kahlil Gibran and Rod McKuen' (251), a judgement which pleases Joan enormously. Certainly, Atwood leaves us much room for doubt about the education and tastes of her heroine.

Arthur as film hero is a projection of Joan's solipsistic psyche as surely as is her mother and everyone else in the novel. Like the speaker in the poems in *Power Politics*, Joan is a Dr Frankenstein who has lost contol of her art. Unlike Joan, however, the speaker in the poems faces the consequences and accepts at least partial responsibility for what she creates: 'They were all inaccurate:/the hinged bronze man, the fragile man/built of glass pebbles,/the fanged man with his opulent capes and boots. . . . It was my fault but you helped,/you enjoyed it' (*Selected Poems*, 176). Joan herself is all the wives of Bluebeard, and Arthur, like the lover in 'Hesitations outside the Door', is created as the mass murderer, around his head a 'crown/of shining blood' (*Selected Poems*, 169). The speaker in the poem, finally, must enter the secret chamber, must confront a reality that all the fictions do not disguise: 'In the room we will find nothing/In the room we will find each other' (*Selected Poems*, 172). It is doubtful that Joan achieves a similar confrontation.

The ending of *Lady Oracle*, as is the case with all of Atwood's fiction, is ambiguous: the reader is not granted the expected resolution. Joan does not learn the lesson so crucial to the speaker in 'Hesitations outside the Door'; perhaps she does not even enter the secret room. Like the protagonist of *Surfacing*, Joan lives in 'border country', trapped between alternatives, unable to make decisions. From the beginning of the novel, Joan has trembled on thresholds, hesitated outside doors, been terrified to cross bridges. Things happen *to* her, and, at least in her imagination, nothing is her fault. Her very birth, according to her mother, is an 'accident', and so decisions are irrelevant in such a fated existence. Joan never exercises the great existential NO in her dealings with men and women, but rather waits 'for something to happen, the next turn of events (a circle? a spiral?)' (342). Her self-created maze represents, not revelation and discovery, but a mere plot device: '. . . in any labyrinth I would have let go of the thread in order to follow a wandering light, a fleeting voice' (170). Even if she enters the secret room, she does not confront its significance: 'In a fairy tale I would be one of the two stupid sisters who open the forbidden door and are shocked by the murdered wives, not the third, clever one who keeps to the essentials: presence of mind, foresight, the telling of watertight lies' (170).

Truth does not translate into art nor art into truth for Joan, as Atwood always indicates that it must. Joan resolves at the end of the novel to abandon her costume Gothics because 'I think they were bad for me' (379), but she will make a poor substitution in the form of science fiction, merely another kind of romance. 'I keep thinking I should learn some lesson from all of this', Joan says, but the reader's hopes for her regeneration are not rewarded. Of her life and her staged death, she says, 'It did make a mess; but then, I don't think I'll ever be a very tidy person' (380).

Nor is *Lady Oracle* intended to be a 'tidy' novel. As Atwood says, '. . . the book I set out to write was a kind of antithesis to *Surfacing*, which is very tight and everything in it fits and there's not anything that's out of place and no tangents. . . . In *Lady Oracle* I set out to write a book that was all tangents'.[3] If, as many critics have noted and as Atwood herself has said, *Lady Oracle* is an 'anti-Gothic' novel, a satire on the conventions of the nineteenth-century romances which Atwood discusses in *Second Words*, then perhaps the novel's lack of resolution is part of that satiric intent. Certainly, Joan is a parody of the Gothic heroine who, according to Judith McCombs in 'Atwood's Haunted Sequences', is '. . . tempted by male Others whose power animates and captivates, whose guises enthrall, whose love spells death'.[4]

But Joan is nothing if not a survivor. She may imagine

demon lovers, but she will run for her life if they actually appear. Joan's Gothic novels thus function like her other lies and like her fat lady disguise: they protect her from 'what is in the room', from a reality she wishes to avoid. She prefers Arthur as Linton rather than as a '. . . cloaked, sinuous and faintly menacing stranger'; she is safe, she rationalises, because '. . . cloaked strangers didn't leave their socks on the floor or stick their fingers in their ears or gargle in the morning to kill germs. I kept Arthur in our apartment and the strangers in their castles and mansions, where they belonged' (241). Thus, largely because of Joan's talents for survival, *Lady Oracle* is essentially a comic work. According to Clara Thomas, who sees Joan as an archetypal 'fool-heroine', the novel is '. . . written with a light touch and to analyze it in other and academic language is inevitably to desecrate it. This is a funny book and we are carried along on the crests of its fun with all the buoyancy of swimming in salt water'.[5]

However, like all great comedy, *Lady Oracle* has a dark side, an aspect recognised by Robert Lecker who writes that its function is to 'corrupt the prototypical romance movement from descent to ascent by demonstrating that the upper world is merely a reflection of the lower world of darkness, ambiguity and isolation'.[6] Joan remains isolated in her tower of false art, victimised by her self-created mythologies. Finally, she is helpless to extricate herself from the threads of her own tapestry, nor can she accept that reality which the mirror reflects. Her only recognition of consequence is that she is 'an escape artist . . . the real romance of my life was that between Houdini and his ropes and locked trunk; entering the embrace of bondage, slithering out again. What else had I ever done' (367). But even this recognition is perhaps an illusion: Joan does not escape her own greatest enemy, which is herself. Funny as she is, Joan shares the essentially tragic position of the

woman writer portrayed in 'Gothic Letter on a Hot Night',
who lives only through her fictions:

> . . . It was the addiction
> to stories, every
> story about herself or anyone
> led to the sabotage of each address
> and all those kidnappings
>
> Stories that could be told
> on nights like these to account for the losses,
> litanies of escapes, bad novels, thrillers
> deficient in villains;
> now there is nothing to write . . . .
>
> Who knows what stories
> would ever satisfy her
> who knows what savageries
> have been inflicted on her
> and others by herself and others
> in the name of freedom,
> in the name of paper. (*You are Happy*, 15–16)

# 5 'The Roar of the Boneyard': *Life Before Man*

Who locked me
into this crazed man-made
stone brain
where the weathered
totempole jabs a blunt
finger at the byzantine
mosaic dome

Under that ornate
golden cranium I wander
among fragments of gods, tarnished
coins, embalmed gestures
chronologically arranged,
looking for the exit sign
but in spite of the diagrams
at every corner, labelled
in red: YOU ARE HERE
the labyrinth holds me.

★　★　★　★

and I am dragged to the mind's
deadend, the roar of the bone-
yard, I am lost

among the mastodons
and beyond. . . . (*The Animals in That Country*, 20)

Although written at least ten years before her novel *Life
Before Man*, Atwood's nightmare poem 'A Night in the
Royal Ontario Museum' is a companion piece. Both poem
and novel centre on the museum as a metaphor for modern
life, which Atwood sees here as a vast tomb or an elaborate
labyrinth, a maze in which human beings are lost,
entrapped, looking for the EXIT sign. All the maps are
obsolete, tradition is no longer a guide, and mirrors have
lost their magic power to reveal truth. Pervasive in the
novel, as in the poem, is a sensation of panic at
the possibility of madness, of being 'dragged to the
mind's/deadend'. And always there is the realisation of
inevitable death, the sand running through the 'glass body'
(*Life Before Man*, 78).

Unlike *Lady Oracle*, *The Edible Woman* or even *Surfacing*,
*Life Before Man* is almost unrelieved by humour except in
its most ironic form. The three protagonists – Lesje,
Elizabeth and Nate – live relentlessly depressing lives, their
states of mind reflected by a surreal cityscape characterised
either by intense heat and the smog of pollution or by
leaden skies and 'fish-grey' snow. Dominating the novel as
it dominates the lives of the protagonists, is the forbidding
image of the Royal Ontario Museum, that grey monument
to an irretrievable past, a temple of death, a massive
'animal morgue' (55). Lesje, who spends her life cataloguing
pieces of bone and teeth, 'shards of the real world', winds
her way through the labyrinth of hallways and exhibits:

She climbs the grey steps of the Museum, walks past
the ticket-takers, hurries up the stairs to the Hall of
Vertebrate Evolution, tracing again her daily path:
the human skull, the saber-toothed cat in its tar pit,
the illuminated scenes of undersea life, with their

> hungry mosasaurs and doomed ammonites. The
> door that leads to her office is reached through this
> portion of the ancient sea floor. (191)

The biblical quotation written across the domed 'golden cranium' of the lobby, 'THAT ALL MEN MAY KNOW HIS WORK' (54), is surely ironic in the context of Atwood's study in extinction.

The characters in this novel are also, like the stuffed dinosaurs and mastodons in the museum, classified and catalogued. Nate, Lesje and Elizabeth are scientifically categorised and arranged in chapters as on file cards, according to name, date, habitat and present activity: 'Elizabeth is lying in bed . . .', 'Nate sits in the Selby Hotel . . .', 'Lesje is doing something seedy . . .'. The impersonal and objective third-person narrator, scientist-like, makes no evaluative comments; the lives of the three protagonists are simply the subjects of a report covering a representative two-year period from Friday, 29 October 1976 to Friday, 18 August 1978. Often a single date is repeated, as the activities and perceptions of the subjects on that date will differ; occasionally there is a flashback to 1975, at which point another major character, Chris, shot his head off.

The reader is not invited to empathise with any of the characters; none is likable or perhaps even redeemable. We remain detached yet fascinated as they interact. As Lesje passes her time wondering about the breeding habits of various dinosaurs, so we view the behaviour of the subjects in the novel: there are two suicides, three contemplated suicides, two faked suicides, two funerals, two rapes, numerous seductions, abundant mental cruelty. None of the sexual acts is even vaguely erotic. Rather Atwood gives us case histories, records of 'sex among the ossified' (128). The characters are fossils of human beings, guilty of 'embalmed gestures', incapable of love and spiritually exhausted. Atwood's poem, 'Letters', explores a similar set of characteristics: 'I do not know/the manner of your deaths, daily/or final, blood/will not flow in the fossil/heart at my command, I can't/put the life back into those/lives, those lies . . .' (*Two-Headed Poems*, 31).

As the characters are classified within the structure of the novel, so they attempt to classify and categorise each other, fit each other neatly into labelled boxes. Lesje attempts to relate to Nate, 'Elizabeth's husband, the husband belonging to Elizabeth. Possessive, or, in Latin, genitive' (53). Nate is, indeed, Elizabeth's husband, father to Nancy and Janet, lover to Lesje, father to Lesje's unborn baby, former lover to Martha, son to Mrs Schoenhof and to a father dead in World War II, former lawyer turned toy-maker, former idealist turned cynic. Tall, thin, bearded, shabby, having only recently discarded his love-beads, Nate is a refugee from the 1960s lost in the maze of the 70s, homesick for his own youth. Nate has no actual home, we are repeatedly made aware; the house he lives in belongs to Elizabeth, even though it is Nate who cleans and cooks and mothers the children. He cooks liver and plays his Harry Belafonte records from the 60s, two activities hateful to Elizabeth, only when Elizabeth is not at home. Later, he moves to Lesje's apartment, where he also cooks and cleans and mothers Lesje. Always he is nostalgic for a home, an impossible and absurd vision of a '. . . shared harmonious life, left over from some Christmas card of the forties, a log fire, knitting in a basket, glued on snow . . .' (212). Ironically, 'Schoenhof' translates from the German as 'beautiful farm'.

Nate cleans and cooks and serves women out of a prevailing and intense sense of guilt, guilt because his surname is German (the protagonist of *Surfacing* at one point remarks, 'The trouble some people have being German I have being human'), because he cannot live up to the heroic image he has of the father he never met, and, more acutely, because he is male in what for him is a female world. Nate is, in fact, terrified of the women who dominate his life. Raised by a mother who is a dedicated if ineffectual political activist, Nate is guilty for failing in his role as 'radical lawyer', defender of the oppressed. Married to Elizabeth, 'Queen Elizabeth', who will 'stop at nothing. Or, put another way: when she reaches nothing she will stop' (133), Nate only tolerates her lovers and serves her tea in bed. He has imagined her at her office in the Royal Ontario Museum, 'sitting like a Madonna in a shrine, shedding a quiet light . . . . He would think of himself running towards her as she receded in front of him, holding a lamp in her hand like Florence Nightingale'. Even when Nate has become disenchanted, even when he realises that Elizabeth is less the 'lady with the lamp' than 'the lady with the axe' (41), he still runs towards her, seeking approval, seeking absolution. Nor can he expect forgiveness from his two daughters who will soon be women, 'and that recognition runs through him like a needle. . . . they will criticize his clothes, his job, his turn of phrase. . . . they will judge him. Motherless, childless, he sits at the kitchen table, the solitary wanderer, under the cold red stars' (265).

Absolution is what Nate also hopes from Lesje, 'Our Lady of the Bones' (71), 'unattainable, shining like a crescent moon' (115). Nate's sexual fantasies about Lesje, as about all women, are firmly grounded in arrested adolescence, having to do with his viewing of the film *She* 'when he was an impressionable twelve and masturbating nightly' (62). He imagines the following scenario:

> Holding Lesje would be like holding some strange
> plant, smooth, thin, with sudden orange flowers.
> *Exotics*, the florists called them. The light would be
> odd, the ground underfoot littered with bones. Over
> which she would have power. She would stand

before him, the bearer of healing wisdom, swathed
in veils. He would fall to his knees, dissolve. (62)

However, as Atwood points out in her essay 'Superwoman
Drawn and Quartered: The Early Forms of *She*', the
image of 'She' is associated by H. Rider Haggard in his
novel, with 'She-Who-Must-Be-Obeyed' (*Second Words*,
38). Like all the women in Nate's experience, even the
innocent young Lesje turns out to be manipulative and
domineering, yet another 'lady with an axe'. Like Elizabeth
and Martha, Lesje also requires that Nate grow up, accept
the role of fatherhood, commit himself to her, return to his
legal career, abandon his toys. Nate, however, remains a
child, unable to truly commit himself to any person or
thing. In imagery typical of Atwood's earlier descriptions
of failed artists, Nate sees himself as divided, amputated,
his own toys effigies of himself: 'The head screwed on,
holding the man together. A clown's smile he used. This is
his body, stiff fragments held together by his spine and his
screwtop head. Segmented man' (223).

Clearly Nate nurtures a vision of himself as victim; like
the female protagonists of Atwood's earlier fiction, he uses
this sense of himself to mitigate his guilt, to absolve himself
of complicity in the violence which he sees as implicit in
sexual relationships in general. Yet, he is an accomplice, at
least in his imagination: he envisions Elizabeth in the grip
of her maddened lover, beaten and helpless, 'white flesh
buckling under those fists, powerless, whimpering', but
the vision is 'only momentarily erotic' (214). Nate creates
Chris as the male monster, an alternate self permitted the
excesses which Nate represses in himself. Imagining Chris
as the brutal rapist and savage beast enables Nate to remain
the chaste knight in the service of his ladies, a role which
renders him psychologically and sometimes physically
impotent, always ineffectual. He thinks of himself in terms

of 'a lump of putty, helplessly molded by the relentless demands and flinty disapprovals of the women he can't help being involved with' (33). Like numerous other of Atwood's characters, Nate is an 'escape artist', but a failed one. His obsessive jogging only traps him more hopelessly within the labyrinth as he runs in circles around Toronto's Parliament Buildings, running from women, from himself, for his life: 'His shadow paces him, thin and pinheaded, stretching away to his right, a blackness flickering over the grass. A premonition, always with him; his own eventual death' (287).

Elizabeth also is preoccupied with death. Those chapters of which Elizabeth is the subject frequently open with her lying on her bed, arms at her sides, staring at the ceiling, simulating death. Her carefully-decorated parlour, in which she frequently sits 'as if waiting for a plane' (15), is funereal in its atmosphere. The walls and furniture are a uniform grey/mushroom colour, devoid of personality and of light save for a quality of 'underwater light'. She derives most pleasure from the two porcelain bowls on the sideboard, 'good pieces', but empty, without use: '. . . they were meant for offerings. Right now they hold their own space, their own beautifully shaped absence' (16). Elizabeth is also an absence, mechanically eating and bathing, 'servicing' her body 'for the time when she may be able to use it again, inhabit it' (74). Within the scope of the novel, such a time does not arrive.

Elizabeth is also concerned about the actual and possible deaths of others. Her two daughters, she fears, could disappear, could 'drown in two inches of water', could die in any number of terrible and bizarre ways. She repeatedly dreams that she is searching for her missing babies through deserted streets, but she knows that the lost babies in the dreams are also her mother, burned to death in a drunken stupor by the fire started from her own cigarette, and her sister, Caroline, who, mad since childhood, drowned herself in a bathtub. These ghosts preoccupy her: 'She's shut them out, both of them, as well as she could, but they come back anyway, using the forms that will most torment her' (171). Equally persistent is the ghost of her former lover, Chris, whose suicide is the ostensible reason for her present severe depression. Elizabeth must also endure yet another death, that of her seemingly indestructible and witch-like foster mother, Auntie Muriel, who is dying of cancer.

Elizabeth's demons, both real and symbolic, haunt her throughout the novel. The opening pages depict the children's preparations for Hallowe'en, but even this image of innocence becomes sinister as the little girls perform 'some grotesque and radical form of brain surgery' (28) on their pumpkins; one of them dresses as a devil. Other children come to the door, disguised as Frankenstein's monsters or as rats; to Elizabeth they represent 'All souls. Not just friendly souls but all souls. They are souls, come back, crying at the door, hungry, mourning their lost lives. You give them food, money, anything to substitute for your love and blood, hoping it will be enough, waiting for them to go away' (45). Predictably, the next holiday recorded in the novel is Remembrance Day, set aside in memory of the dead.

Elizabeth resurrects her demons out of guilt, a guilt which seems a great deal more justifiable than Nate's self-indulgent suffering. She understands that her mother died as if by her own hand, that her mother, in fact, had 'sold' her two little daughters to Auntie Muriel. Yet the mother's death is also somehow due to Elizabeth's rejection and denial, her refusal to recognise her mother as the pathetic figure beneath the street lamp, gazing hungrily up at the window of her daughters' bedroom. Elizabeth has also prevented the younger Caroline from reconciliation with the mother and has thus contributed to Caroline's tragic breakdown and eventual death. On the night that Caroline symbolically leaves her body, enters into a state of catatonic collapse, Elizabeth has left her alone in order to seek her own thrills and lose her virginity to a boy she picks up on the street. She has also precipitated Chris's death by refusing to marry him, by ordering him from her house. Even the death of the evil Auntie Muriel is somehow partly her fault: she has hurled one of her precious bowls at Auntie Muriel, who has melted as a result. Lying in the hospital, the cancer consuming her body, Auntie Muriel appears to be 'falling in on herself, she's melting, like the witch in *The Wizard of Oz*, and seeing it Elizabeth remembers: Dorothy was not jubilant when the witch turned into a puddle of brown sugar. She was terrified' (258).

Perhaps Elizabeth's guilt is, in a convoluted way, responsible for her punishment of others, punishments almost as cruel as those she metes out to herself. She is the sadist in the sado-masochistic relationship with both Nate and Chris, the long leather gloves she wears and removes so deliberately, finger by finger, an emblem of her role. All her sexual relationships, which she interprets as tests of her dominance and power, manifest forms of perversity. Her parlour becomes a kind of web into which she seduces such victims as William, Lesje's lover before Nate. According to Elizabeth, William is comparable in bed to 'a large and fairly active slab of Philadelphia cream cheese', but he may also contain 'pockets of energy, even violence' (196), an accurate interpretation as we know from Lesje's experience of William. The real challenge for Elizabeth, however, has been Chris, 'a dangerous country, swarming with ambushes and guerrillas, the center of a whirlpool, a demon lover' (196). Even Elizabeth's youthful escapades are flirtations with rape and violence; her adult forays into sleazy bars are equally degrading and dangerous. While Marian in *The Edible Woman* only fantasises about 'the Underwear Man', Elizabeth actually arranges a date with a travelling salesman of fetishistic underwear for women. 'We both know what you're here for' (209), he says just before he rapes a now-frigid Elizabeth while holding the microphone of his two-way radio against her throat in order to give his listeners 'a thrill'.

There is also an element of voyeurism in Elizabeth's relationships with Nate's lovers. She invites their confidences and confessions, and her manipulation of both Martha and Lesje is almost sexual in its cruelty. Again, Elizabeth is the Spider Woman who invites the innocent flies into her parlour, takes them to lunch, snickers as they spill their coffee and expose their weaknesses. Lesje is not so terribly erroneous in her classification of Elizabeth as 'CLASS: *Chondrichthyes*; ORDER: *Selachii*; GENUS: *Squalidae*; SPECIES: *Elizabetha*. Today she classifies Elizabeth as a shark; on other days it's as a huge Jurassic toad, primitive, squat, venomous; on other days a cephalopod, a giant squid, soft and tentacled, with a hidden beak' (245).

As always, however, Atwood does not permit her readers such a simple interpretation of character. Elizabeth cannot be so easily categorised and dismissed. For one thing, she is subject to unexpected expressions of tenderness, towards her children especially, but also towards Auntie Muriel, whom she has good reason to hate. At their last encounter in the hospital, Elizabeth wishes to run, to leave Auntie Muriel to the fate she deserves, but she recalls her mother's death, and the good, the vulnerable part of her prevents her flight:

> . . . she leans forward and takes Auntie Muriel's blinded hands. Desperately the stubby fingers clutch her. Elizabeth is no priest: she cannot give absolution. What can she offer? Nothing sincerely. Beside her own burning mother she has sat, not saying anything, holding the one good hand. The one good fine-boned hand. The ruined hand, still beautiful, unlike the veined and mottled stumps she now cradles in hers,

soothing them with her thumbs as in illness she has
soothed the hands of her children.

Sickness grips her. Nevertheless, nevertheless, she
whispers: It's all right. It's all right. (260)

A similar gesture, that of touching, will prove the salvation
of the protagonist of *Bodily Harm*.

Elizabeth is like Auntie Muriel in many ways,
domineering, spiteful, with 'the backbone of a rhinoceros'.
Yet there is a positive aspect to Elizabeth's strengths. She
is a survivor, a 'homemaker' in a world where homes are
not possible. Literally homeless in childhood while the
other characters in *Life Before Man* are only symbolically
homeless, Elizabeth has created, by the end of the novel, a
home against all the odds. She will go to her home and
make peanut butter sandwiches for her children:

> It suddenly amazes her that she is able to do this,
> something this simple. How close has she come,
> how many times, to doing what Chris did? More
> important: what stopped her?
>     . . . But she's still alive, she wears clothes, she
> walks around, she holds down a job even. She has
> two children. Despite the rushing of wind, the
> summoning voices she can hear from underground,
> the dissolving trees, the chasms that open at her feet;
> and will always from time to time open. She has no
> difficulty seeing the visible world as a transparent
> veil or a whirlwind. The miracle is to make it solid.
>     She thinks with anticipation of her house, her
> quiet living room with its empty bowls, pure grace,
> her kitchen table. Her house is not perfect; parts of
> it are in fact crumbling, most noticeably the front
> porch. But it's a wonder that she has a house at all,
> that she's managed to accomplish a house. Despite
> the wreckage. She's built a dwelling over the abyss,

but where else was there to build it? So far, it
stands. (278)

In the final analysis, Elizabeth is the only adult in the
novel. She has, as she says, 'been down the yellow brick
road' (86), and she knows well enough that the Wizard
does not exist. Her own escape fantasy, inspired by Chinese
paintings she commissions for a showing at the museum,
involves the idealisation of peasant life, the intensely
artificial beauty of fruit and vegetables, the sentimental
assertion that 'Everyone Helps in Building each Others'
Houses'. But Elizabeth knows that no one helps, that
'paradise does not exist', that the Chinese paintings do not
represent reality but only desire: 'Like cavemen, they paint
not what they see but what they want' (291). Elizabeth is
not an heroic figure in any ordinary sense, but she is strong
in her loneliness, ready to face a reality that is unmitigatedly
hostile. She resolves the existential dilemma evaded by all
of Atwood's earlier heroines: she has pitted her own free
will against the absurd, and she survives.

Lesje, on the other hand, is one of Atwood's more
familiar perennial child/women, and, as Lesje classifies her
fossils, other people, and the world in general, so we are
tempted to classify *her* among Atwood's Diana figures
patterned after the archetypes discussed in *Survival*. Like
Marian in *The Edible Woman* and like Alice in Wonderland,
Lesje avoids growing up or confronting reality by becoming
a tourist 'underground'. Lesje's chapters, including the
first one of which she is the subject, frequently describe
her wandering through the Jurassic swamp of her
imagination: she is in prehistory, 'Under a sun more orange
than her own has ever been, in the middle of a swampy
plain lush with thick-stalked plants and oversized ferns, a
group of bony-plated stegosaurs is grazing. . . . She mixes
eras, adds colors: why not a metallic blue stegosaurus with
red and yellow dots . . . ?' (10). Lesje is a paleontologist, a

scientist, compulsively objective just as Joan Foster in
*Lady Oracle* is compulsively romantic. Yet Lesje's views on
prehistory are derived from the imagination rather than
from textbooks. Her 'passion for fossils' originates with her
reading of Sir Arthur Conan Doyle's *The Lost World* when
she was ten, and she has never outgrown the idea that, like
the hero of the novel, she might also discover some lost
world in which prehistoric life survives.

When that event occurs, as she still imagines it inevitably
will, she will name her country after herself, a plan which
poses a problem because, also like Joan Foster, Lesje has
multiple names. Her last name would have been Etlin had
not her Ukrainian grandfather changed it to Green when
he arrived in Canada, and 'There already was a Greenland,
which wasn't at all the sort of place she had in mind.
Greenland was barren, icy, devoid of life, whereas the
place Lesje intended to discover would be tropical, rich
and crawling with wondrous life forms . . .' (82). Lesje is
Ukrainian for Alice, a name Lesje uses for a time, but she
finally prefers Lesje because 'Aliceland' simply 'wasn't
right'. Nevertheless, Atwood here establishes her familiar
theme: Lesje is another Alice travelling in a 'green world'
of her own creation.

Although Lesje's fantasies are redolent with lush sexual
imagery – steaming swamps, phallic shapes, dinosaurs with
two penises – and although she spends an inordinate
amount of time musing on the sexual habits of her
prehistoric creatures – the 'gargantuan passions, the earth
actually moving . . . sighs of lust like a full-blast factory
whistle' (128) – these fantasies actually represent an evasion
of sex in any real context. Lesje is not a participant in life,
prehistoric or otherwise, but a voyeur watching from
behind a large fern, 'invisible' to the dinosaurs to whom
she is 'so totally alien that they will not be able to focus on
her. When the aborigines sighted Captain Cook's ships,
they ignored them because they knew such things could

not exist. It's the next best thing to being invisible' (10). As the heroine of *Surfacing* prays to be made invisible, as Joan Foster in *Lady Oracle* regards her excess weight as 'a magic cloak of invisibility', and as Marian in *The Edible Woman* seeks to disappear by refusing to eat, so Lesje in this novel finds it convenient to temporarily eliminate herself.

Invisibility in Atwood's terms, is a complex symbol: at times, it represents a refusal to deal with reality, a means of escape from a necessary confrontation, but invisibility is also the prerogative of the artist. Atwood writes in *Second Words* that one of the things she used to wish for when she was very young 'and reading a lot of comic books and fairy tales', was 'the cloak of invisibility, so I could follow people around and listen to what they were saying when I wasn't there . . .'. This is what novelists do, says Atwood, 'every time they write a page' (*Second Words*, 429). But, like Joan Foster and Marian McAlpin, Lesje may have the soul of an artist, but she misuses and misinterprets her talents. Like other of Atwood's heroines, she is a 'failed artist', solipsistic and incapable of translating the imagination into language. To remain invisible in the green world is to escape 'real life', adulthood, the sexual recognition that implies, and the moral implications of the role of artist as well.

For Lesje, 'men replaced dinosaurs, true, in her head as in geological time; but thinking about men has become too unrewarding' (11). The men in Lesje's life are in fact remarkably unrewarding. At first she lives with William, who is a double to Peter in *The Edible Woman*, a 'good man', theoretically safe but unutterably boring. 'William Wasp', as Lesje thinks of him, is 'pink-cheeked' and 'hairless' (20), and an incurable optimist who believes that 'every catastrophe is merely a problem looking for a brilliant solution' (19). William, he and Lesje both believe, will save the world in his professional capacity as a specialist in environmental engineering, translate 'sewage disposal':

'. . . they're all in danger of drowning in their own shit. William will save them. You can see it just by looking at him, his confidence, his enthusiasm' (19).

But, as is almost always the case in Atwood's novels and poems, beneath the clean white shirt beats the heart of a Bluebeard; the facade of an Albert Schweitzer hides the reality of a Hitler; the redeemer inevitably becomes the infamous Underwear Man. Elizabeth has recognised those 'pockets of violence' latent in William, but Lesje is shocked to find herself raped, violated: 'She always thought of rape as something the Russians did to the Ukrainians, something the Germans did, more furtively, to the Jews; something blacks did in Detroit, in dark alleys. But not something William Wasp, from a good family in London, Ontario, would ever do to her' (169). Like the naive narrator in Atwood's short story, 'Rape Fantasies', who believes that rape always happens to someone else and is an event that might be avoided by simply reasoning with the rapist, Lesje does not even know what to call William's act of violence. 'The incident', nevertheless, is traumatic enough to precipitate Lesje's departure from their apartment, paving the way for her intensified relationship with Nate.

Whereas William regards Lesje as racially suspect, her Ukrainian-Jewish heritage rendering her unfit in his judgement to meet his parents or bear his child, Nate is attracted to what he considers exotic in Lesje. And Lesje is attracted to Nate *because* he sees her as exotic: 'the fact is that she's addicted to Nate's version of her. . . . she wants to be this beautiful phantom, this boneless wraith he's conjured up. Sometimes she really does want it' (247). Lesje is, of course and with good reason, terrified of Elizabeth, and yet there is a perverse desire on her part to 'become' Elizabeth, a thing she can best accomplish by marrying Nate: '. . . she wants to belong, to be seen to belong; she wants to be classifiable, a member of a group. There is already a group of Mrs Schoenhofs: one is Nate's mother, the other is the mother of his children' (246). Lesje considers that 'maybe she's been thinking too much about Elizabeth. . . . If she isn't careful she'll turn into Elizabeth' (247).

In significant ways, Lesje does just this. Whether it is Nate's necessity to create domineering women in order to absolve his guilt, or whether Lesje is innately this and her role of ingenue is merely a disguise, she begins more and more to resemble Elizabeth. Her first sexual experience with Nate takes place in Elizabeth's bed, and her later evaluations of Nate reflect Elizabeth's perceptions: he becomes for her an object of ridicule, an object to be possessed and used. Her very language takes on the qualities of Elizabeth's hard-edged tone: Lesje tells Nate, 'I've got news for you . . . . Elizabeth doesn't need any support. Elizabeth needs support like a nun needs tits' (268). Lesje comes to regard Nate with 'ball-shriveling looks', as if 'he was a teeny little dog turd' (237). And, she begins to understand Nate's real value in terms that were Elizabeth's as well: he can provide a classification for her; he can make her a mother.

Atwood's great fertility myth as a symbol of rebirth and artistic creativity, as it figures so prominently in all her novels and in so many of her poems, is completely inverted in *Life Before Man*. In a doomed world, its inhabitants on the verge of extinction, even childbirth becomes an ironic commentary, a mockery of artistic and biological creativity. Lesje's act of throwing away her birth control pills, an act of liberation for the protagonist of *Surfacing*, is here committed in revenge and with malice. 'Surely no child conceived in such a rage could come to much good', Lesje worries. 'She would have a throwback, a reptile, a mutant of some kind with scales and a little horn on the snout' (270).

Lesje herself, however, is the real monster. Earlier she has identified herself as a 'herbivore', peaceful and benign. But Lesje's teeth, a feature she comments upon at various points in the novel, are too big; they indicate an ominous hunger. On the morning following the conception of her baby, Lesje is 'gnawing a bran muffin, hair falling over her face'; she looks at Nate 'like Fate, sullen, gauging'. She wants him to know that she has not been 'caged' (270). Three months later, her pregnancy confirmed but Nate still unnotified, Lesje imagines locking herself into one of the museum's display cases, 'hairy mask on her face, she'll stow away, they'll never get her out' (284). Always one of Atwood's 'dancing girls', Lesje is, at the end of the novel, still dancing, this time among the carnivores: 'Here are her old acquaintances, familiar to her as pet rabbits: allosaurus, the carnivore, parrot-beaked chasmosaurus, parasaurolophus with its deer-antler crest' (285). She joins a bizarre parade: '. . . one after another the fossils would lift their ponderous feet, moving off along the grove of resurrected trees, flesh coalescing like ice or mist around them. They'd dance stumpily down the stairs of the Museum and out the front door' (286).

Nate may imagine that he has found a home with Lesje (although his continued presence at the Selby Hotel bar would indicate otherwise), but Lesje at the end is wearing her white coat, symbol, not of wifehood, but of her perennial 'virginity' and of her status as museum employee, as scientist. The white coat is Lesje's 'label' for herself, her need for labels being analogous to Nate's search for a home. Throughout the novel, Lesje longs for an identity, a label, a category to which to belong. She wishes she were either Ukrainian or Jewish and not a combination of the two, not 'multicultural'. She tries on fashionable clothes in the stores, but cannot determine into which style of fashion she fits. She decides, finally, that the 'Mrs. Schoenhof' label is not compatible with her role as scientist: 'a pregnant paleontologist is surely a contradiction in terms. Her business is the naming of bones, not the creation of flesh' (284). Her real home then is the museum: 'She does belong here. . . . This is the only membership she values' (283). None of these convictions represents a favourable sign for the success of Lesje's possible marriage to Nate or for the positive symbolism of her future motherhood. Lesje's labels, like the polar thinking in terms of good and evil on the part of the protagonist of *Surfacing*, entrap her in the realm of childhood. She remains, at least psychologically, among the guardians of death, a permanent resident yet still a tourist in an ideal world in which the only life is 'a life before man'.

The greater number of Atwood scholars would not agree with the above interpretation of Lesje's pregnancy and the novel's final resolution. Linda Hutcheon in 'From Poetic to Narrative Structures: The Novels of Margaret Atwood' sees Lesje's pregnancy as a 'truly creative act' which becomes 'the real paradigm of the novelist's act of creation, an act of moral responsibility for the creation of life'.[1] Frank Davey also concludes that Lesje discards her birth control pills 'in order to claim her future'.[2] Such evaluations are based, understandably, on an accurate interpretation of Atwood's use of fertility symbolism in earlier novels. However, *Life Before Man* marks, not so much a change in Atwood's literary directions, as an intensification of her ironic sensibility and of her political consciousness. Sherrill Grace's predictions in *Violent Duality* that this novel represents 'what may prove to be a new stage in Atwood's artistic evolution', that of 'social and domestic realism',[3] were indeed perceptive, although Grace might well have added the term 'political' to describe Atwood's areas of artistic concern.

As I have argued in Chapter 1, Atwood's works have always been 'political' in that they represent a social consciousness, a concern for the survival of individuals, particularly women, in a world characterised by hostility and violence that is both latent and overt. *The Edible Woman* is a study of the evils of a consumer society as well

as of the psychology of young womanhood; beneath the
narrative of *Surfacing* and *The Journals of Susanna Moodie*
is a pervading sense of the violation of nature and a concern
for ecological balance. In *Life Before Man*, such concerns
become paramount: for Atwood, the human race may
indeed be confronting its own extinction, its own mass
suicide.

The characters in this novel are in fact homeless, for one
major reason: their world is no longer habitable. William's
sanitation efforts are absurdly futile, but at least he makes
an attempt to salvage what is possible. His gloomy
predictions are annoying to Lesje, and, through her
perceptions, we too see William as a joke. Atwood's jokes,
however, are almost inevitably laced with a deadly irony,
and, as is often the case in her fiction, the least likely
character becomes a speaker of truth. William serves as
both fool and prophet in the following passages:

> . . . pollutants are pouring into the air, over three
> hundred of them, more than have yet been identified.
> Sulfuric acid and mercury are falling, metallic mist,
> acid rain, into the pure lakes of Muskoka and points
> north. Queasy fish rise, roll over, exposing bellies
> soon to bloat. If ten times more control is not
> implemented at once (at once!) the Great Lakes will
> die. A fifth of the fresh water in the world. And for
> what? Panty-hose . . . rubber bands, cars, plastic
> buttons . . . .

> . . . birds are eating worms, and stable, unbreakable
> PCB's are concentrating in their fatty tissues. Lesje
> herself has probably been incapacitated for safe child-
> bearing due to the large quantity of DDT she has
> already stored in her own fatty tissues. Not to
> mention the radiation bombardment on her ovaries,
> which will almost certainly cause her to give birth to

a two-headed child or to a lump of flesh the size of a
grapefruit, containing hair and a fully developed set
of teeth . . . or to a child with its eyes on one side of
its face, like a flounder. (126)

Not only are human beings violating nature, they are
also violating each other with a similar destructive intensity.
Nate scans the newspaper headlines, and what he sees is
'one long blurred howl of rage and pain':

> . . . the Pakistani pushed onto the subway tracks.
> . . . The child who strangled while being forced by
> her mother to stand on one foot with a rope around
> her neck as punishment. Gossip about Margaret
> Trudeau, for weeks. An exploding butcher's shop in
> Northern Ireland. Widening rift between English
> and French Canada. Murdered Portuguese shoeshine
> boy; cleanup of Toronto's Sin Strip. Quebec
> language laws: Greek grocers in all-Greek districts
> forbidden to put up Coca-Cola signs in Greek. (184)

'What else can be expected', Nate asks himself, and his
own impotence is confirmed in his vision of the newspapers
as studies in 'distilled futility'. Language itself, at this
point in Atwood's literary philosophy, is suspect, often
futile; 'the true story is vicious/and multiple and
untrue/after all . . .', Atwood writes in *True Stories* (11).
Many of the poems in this volume, in *You Are Happy* and
in *Two-Headed Poems* are concerned with the inadequacy
of poetry, of art, in the face of the destruction and atrocity
that constitute reality. How can one write poems or novels
about that which is indescribable? 'How can I justify/this
gentle poem then in the face of sheer/horror?' (*True
Stories*, 34). How does one dare, like Elizabeth, to build a
house over the abyss?

The alternative is to remain silent, to refuse the

confrontation, to hide from reality in fantasy, or to be detached. One of Atwood's great ironic observations about Lesje is that she was named for a famous Ukrainian poet, and yet Lesje either refuses or is unable to speak. She is always 'afraid of saying the wrong thing; of being accused' (53); she is always inept in social situations, and she has no close friends. After their first lunch together, Nate is unable to remember what she said: 'did she even say anything?' (61). For Lesje, the names of rocks are the only meaningful language: 'not many people might know it, but if you found one who did, you would be able to talk together' (83). But the truly monstrous thing about Lesje, Atwood implies, is that she chooses to regard even the inevitable destruction of humankind with scientific detachment. Unlike Nate or even Elizabeth, Lesje chooses to remain emotionally uninvolved: 'the real question is: Does she care whether the human race survives or not? She doesn't know. The dinosaurs didn't survive and it wasn't the end of the world . . . the human race has it coming. Nature will think up something else. Or not, as the case may be' (19).

The human race may indeed 'have it coming', and yet, in Atwood's own terms, it is still possible to care, to forgive and to redeem. Language is a 'fragile protest', but it represents the only salvation possible: '. . . you must write this poem', she says, 'because there is nothing more to do' (*True Stories*, 70). In her next two novels, *Bodily Harm* and *The Handmaid's Tale*, and in her poems, *True Stories*, Atwood writes that poem, the one '. . . that invents nothing/and excuses nothing' (*True Stories*, 70): 'Here is the handful/of shadow I have brought back to you:/this decay, this hope, this mouth-/ful of dirt, this poetry' (*True Stories*, 93).

# 6  Politics and Prophecy: *Bodily Harm*, *The Handmaid's Tale* and *True Stories*

At that moment when the nameless heroine of *Surfacing* walks out of the Canadian forest, brushes the leaves from her matted hair, puts on her clothes and proclaims to herself and the trees that she refuses 'to be a victim', Atwood's subsequent fiction and poetry also begin to emphasise a quality of proclamation. Atwood's principal concern in *Surfacing* and in earlier fiction and poetry has been to delineate the psychological factors of sexual politics, the behaviour of women in conflict with men. But only in the later novels and poems does Atwood expand her political view to encompass a world in which both men and women are caught up in the struggle to see 'who can do what to whom and get away with it, even as far as death' (*Handmaid's Tale*, 144). Oppression in all its manifestations, both physical and psychological, is Atwood's subject in *Bodily Harm* and *The Handmaid's Tale* and in the poems entitled *True Stories*. Both novels and the poetry are profoundly political; all represent the confrontation with power and its universal forms: dictatorship, tyranny, torture and the reality of violence.

The heroines of the novels begin as typical Atwood women; they are not quite so young as earlier protagonists, but like them they protest their own innocence and attempt a withdrawal from circumstances for which they do not accept responsibility. Rennie Wilford of *Bodily Harm* is, like Joan Foster of *Lady Oracle*, 'an escape artist', intent on the evasion of the uncompromising realities that make up her life. Atwood presents these realities as unmitigatedly horrific, for they include a recent mastectomy and the possible death sentence of cancer. Like Atwood's images of amputation discussed in earlier chapters, the mastectomy is symbolic of a psychological separation from the self both as woman and as artist, a division between the actual self and the self one attempts to create, a condition which is potentially as deadly as the cancer. Comparatively less immediately threatening but still problematic are Rennie's persistent memories of a lonely and loveless childhood passed in the small town of 'Griswold', the atmosphere of which is almost as ominous as its name and is surely an inversion of the 'green world' of earlier Atwood fiction. Rennie's other problems include a current lover who enjoys rape games and an actual rapist who has entered her apartment in her absence and left a coiled rope as a calling card. Her job writing trivia for pupil magazines represents a misuse of her talents and is itself a kind of bondage.

The lover and the job, of course, are indications that Rennie has, at least in part, chosen her life. She tolerates the lover's eccentricities, passively accepting his management of her world. She acquiesces while he redecorates her apartment, kills her plants because they don't reflect a concept of modern decor, dictates her clothing, and choreographs their sexual relationship with black lace nightgowns and suggestions of bondage. From the beginning, Rennie abdicates power; she is passive to the point that even Jake loses interest, not so much because of her mastectomy as she believes, but because of her remarkable acceptance of his exploitive behaviour. Rennie reacts to her abandonment with predictable passivity, for it allows her to feel that her victimisation is complete; it reinforces her view of herself as innocent in contrast to a perverse world. She seems almost deliberately to manifest the victim psychology which Atwood announces as her subject in the epigraph to the novel taken from John Berger's *Ways of Seeing*: 'A man's presence suggests what he is capable of doing to you or for you. By contrast, a woman's presence . . . defines what can and cannot be done to her'.

Rennie's job accomplishes a similar end in securing this image of herself as victim. Like earlier Atwood heroines and like some of the Canadian writers whose works Atwood explores in *Survival*, she is a failed artist, deliberately renouncing her responsibility as artist and as human being to confront reality, to search for truth. But Rennie does not choose to *see*. Rather, she concentrates on ephemera, purposefully limiting her assignments to articles on 'relationships' and such fashion trends as 'drain chain jewelry', symbolic, again, of her own emotional bondage. She assiduously avoids the political; Atwood writes, 'Instead of writing about the issues, she began interviewing the people who were involved in them . . . the in wardrobe for the picket line, the importance of the denim overall, what the feminists eat for breakfast' (64). Rennie is most comfortable with short 'pieces' for the 'Swinging Toronto' section of the *Pandora* magazine, although, unlike the Pandora of mythology, she prefers to keep reality under a closed lid: 'I see into the present, that's all . . . Surfaces. There's not a whole lot to it' (26). According to Sherrill Grace in *Violent Duality*, Atwood consistently describes the limitations of *seeing* in '. . . McLuhanesque terms. The exclusive reliance upon the visual sense separates objects in space, splits things off from their contexts, isolates the viewer from the thing viewed. By simply looking *at* something we are able to keep ourselves at a distance, uninvolved.'[1] Rennie is a mistress of remaining uninvolved; her first lesson enforced by her mother back in Griswold had been 'how to look at things without touching them' (54).

When reality is unavoidable, as in the form of personal crises, Rennie seeks to trivialise even these by turning them into 'pieces'. She counters the threat of the anonymous rapist by attempting an article on pornography, a project she abandons when the evidence encountered in her research in a local police station, a photograph of a rat emerging from a vagina, makes her physically ill. Even when Rennie is faced with the medical diagnosis of cancer, she attempts, unsuccessfully, to reduce and thereby escape her experience in the usual way: 'as she walked home she was still thinking in the ways she used to. For instance, she could do a piece on it. "Cancer, The Coming Thing." *Homemakers* might take it, or *Chatelaine*. How about "the Cufoff Point"?' (27).

Rennie again uses her job as an escape route by convincing her editor that she should do a travel article on the Caribbean, an analysis of tennis courts and restaurants. But island paradises, whether actual ones or those of the mind, do not serve Atwood's heroines well, as we know from the preceeding chapters. In *True Stories* Atwood includes a number of poems which reveal the underside of paradise: in 'Postcard', we learn that 'The palm trees on the reverse/are a delusion; so is the pink sand./What we have are the usual/fractured coke bottles and the smell/of backed-up drains, too sweet . . .' (18). In 'Dinner', it is the tourists themselves who dispel any possible magic as they feed '. . . on starch and grease./Engorged buttocks and/thighs jiggle by,/surly soft paunches . . .' (24). Yet there is some element evident that is worse than bad scenery and bad company; just beyond the palms, one catches a glimpse of the cripples and the prisoners, their heads shaved by bayonets. The littered beaches are 'smeared with grease' and 'exhausted lunches' in 'Sunset I', but also with 'clumps of torn-out/hair' (80). In the prose poem, 'True Romances', the ominous becomes the actual:

> They cut off the hands and heads to prevent
> identification but they cannot prevent it. Everyone
> knows who has been shot and thrown into the sea,
> who has been beaten, which man or woman has
> been methodically raped, which left to starve and
> burn in a pit under the noon sun. It's bright there
> and clear, you can see a long way. (*True Stories*, 43)

As is also the case in *Bodily Harm* and in other of Atwood's novels, escape thus becomes unavoidable confrontation. In Rennie's experience, however, the confrontation is with reality of an order so brutal as to seem uncharacteristic for Atwood if we base our judgement on earlier novels. Horrendous heat, glaring sunlight, scorpions, bad food and oil-washed beaches are the least of concerns as Rennie is implicated and involved against her will in a political revolution. She is imprisoned and forced to witness the commission of atrocities; she begins to understand what for Atwood is a crucial point: that no one is 'exempt', even those who have presumably already paid their dues to an illusion of universal justice. The island, Atwood implies, is, like Camus' Algeria, a land of perfect truth, a land which 'casts no shadows' (71). And, in the glare, Rennie watches a series of executions:

> She leans against the wall, she is shaking. It's

indecent, it's not done with ketchup, nothing is
inconceivable here, no rats in the vagina but only
because they haven't though of it yet. . . . Rennie
understands for the first time that this is not
necessarily a place she will get out of, ever. She is
not exempt. Nobody is exempt from anything. (290)

Rennie's situation and experience are foreshadowed in
Atwood's short story, 'A Travel Piece'. Annette, too, writes
travel articles for magazines (as does Atwood herself on
occasion), and her search, like Rennie's, is for an Eden in
the Caribbean, a place in the world, 'where all was well,
where unpleasant things did not happen' (*Dancing Girls*,
131). Annette soon learns that sunny skies and an
'indecently blue ocean' always imply an incongruous reality,
that they are finally 'a giant screen, flat with pictures
painted on it to create the illusion of solidity. If you walked
up to it and kicked it, it would tear and your foot would go
right through, into another space which Annette could
only visualise as darkness, a night in which something she
did not want to look at was hiding' (132). The 'hiding'
thing is, of course, herself and her own failure at
comprehending the realities of her world, her failure at
*seeing*. Atwood arranges the inevitable confrontation before
Annette ever arrives on the island. The plane crashes
somewhere in the Bermuda triangle, and Annette, along
with other passengers, finds herself drifting in a lifeboat.
Unlike the others, however, Annette has been resourceful,
has thought to bring sandwiches and a toothbrush along
with her always-present camera, that instrument which is
always for Atwood a symbol of a failure of vision. Annette
looks at life through a lens, filtering her experience and
thereby distancing herself from it. The camera turns out to
be as useless as the toothbrush, because, as is more and
more the case in Atwood's fiction, the unthinkable occurs;
the group is not rescued, and what had been an orderly and

cooperative attempt at survival quickly degenerates into panic and cannibalism. The story ends with Annette's contemplation of the inhumane behaviour of her comrades as they attempt to slit the throat of a young male passenger. She only watches, concentrating on a numbed sensibility of her own non-involvement, her own innocence. Then there is the vision of the foot through the screen: she *is* involved, and 'this is what it means to be alive. . . . Am I one of them or not?' (143).

Atwood's point in this story, as well as in *Bodily Harm* and in all her previous works, is that we are all somehow guilty of being human and that malignancy is, quite possibly, a metaphor for the human condition. Atwood argues, as she also does at the conclusion of *Surfacing*, for a recognition of and a commitment to that human condition, no matter how malignant, and for an engagement with life, with reality, no matter how brutal or absurd. 'Massive involvement' is for Atwood, and finally for Rennie as well, a term which reflects, not medical pathology, but positive action. The mistaken conviction that 'innocence is merely/not to act', as Atwood writes in 'The Arrest of the Stockbroker', is the ultimate illusion: 'then suddenly you're in there/in this mistake, this stage, this box,/this war grinding across/your body' (*True Stories*, 49). For Atwood, the genteel and the complacent are merely surfaces for the disguise of the horrible; the title of Atwood's prose poem, 'True Romances', implies a terrible irony: 'One of these mornings, when you reach the bottom of your cup, coffee or tea, it could be either, you will look and there will be a severed finger, bloodless, anonymous, a little signal of death sent to you from the foreign country where they grow such things' (*True Stories*, 44). Thus Atwood forces her readers to see beneath surfaces, to confront a kind of reality that is revolutionary as a subject for poetry.

And, no matter how strong her reluctance, Rennie also must look beneath the surfaces, for she is cursed (or finally blessed) with a 'closet honesty' which she before has considered a 'professional liability' (64). She must write about what she sees, and not about what she would like to see, as she is directed by the enigmatic Dr Minnow, for whose acquaintance she has paid the price of imprisonment. Minnow himself pays for his political involvement with his life, and his very name is perhaps indicative of his quasi-religious nature; as Christ is associated symbolically with the image of the fish, so Minnow is, in his way, a minor Christ, embattled against 'Prince', the Prince of Darkness. Given Atwood's by now familiar use of ambiguity, however, Prince might also represent the Prince of Peace, in which case Minnow's role is also reversed. His funeral is like 'some horrible little morality play' in which the expected resurrection fails to occur (250). Even though Atwood has referred to Minnow as 'the one good man in the book' (*Second Words*, 425), there is nevertheless the same enigmatic quality about his symbolic identity that surrounds almost all of her fictional characters. Regardless of how we choose to see him, however, Dr Minnow's earlier sermon to Rennie is exactly what Atwood would like her heroine to hear: '. . . there are still things that are inconceivable', he tells Rennie. 'Here nothing is inconceivable. . . . I wish you to write about it. . . . All I ask you to do is look. . . . Look with your eyes open and you will see the truth of the matter. Since you are a reporter, it is your duty to report' (133–34).

Rennie's woman cellmate in the prison, who has resorted to prostitution for her own and Rennie's survival and who has been brutally beaten, also directs her: 'Tell someone I'm here. . . . Tell someone what happened' (289). To tell, to report, to bear witness, then, is Rennie's moral obligation; by the end of the novel, Rennie realises that she '. . . is a subversive. She was not once but now she is. A reporter. She will pick her time; then she will report' (301). The same necessity, the same indication of political commitment, will also validate the experience of the heroine of *The Handmaid's Tale*. For Atwood, writing itself becomes a political act; the writer is always a reporter of truth, even when her subject is fiction.

In her former self-proclaimed innocence, Rennie has avoided, not only truth in an abstract political sense, but the truth about relationships, between men and women and between women. She has inevitably chosen men who maintain power over her: Daniel, the surgeon who removed her breast and has seen the 'inside' of her and who refuses to sleep with her, manifests one kind of power. He is, in her later dreams, the man with the knife, double to the anonymous would-be rapist. (Interestingly, Annette's husband in 'A Travel Piece' is also a physician, and he too represents a judgemental sort of power. He is a dispenser of tranquilisers, and thus he is responsible for the manipulation of Annette's perceptions.) Paul, the Caribbean adventurer who is either gunrunner or drug smuggler, hero or villain, holds Rennie's very safety in his keeping, and she is almost as self-effacing with him, grateful for his acceptance of her body mutilated by the mastectomy, as she has been with Jake in their destructive long-term relationship. Finally, Rennie comes to realise that all the men in her life are, in reality, one man, and that she herself has chosen him, created him in her own image, his face '. . . familiar, with silver eyes that twin and reflect her own' (287). Always she has been like the malleable women of Atwood's earlier poetry who deliberately subject themselves to rearrangement, even dismemberment, by men who invade them body and soul. Atwood writes in 'Letters, Towards and Away': 'You collapse my house of cards/merely by breathing/. . . and put together my own/body, another/place/for me to live/in' (*The Circle Game*, 85). Again in Atwood's prose poem 'Iconography', a woman submits to every male whim, and for the man in question, 'To make her do something she didn't like and then make her like it, that was the greatest power'. Finally, Atwood advises her selfless and nameless woman of this poem, 'watch yourself. That's what mirrors are for, this story is a mirror story which rhymes with horror story, almost but not quite'. Men are powerful, Atwood concludes the poem, because they have the 'last word', they have, in fact, 'the word' (*Murder in the Dark*, 52).

And through her experiences in the prison and her first-hand apprehension of outrage, Rennie, too, comes to see men in the light of the power they wield, through violence as well as through language: 'She's afraid of men and it's simple, it's rational, she's afraid of men because men are frightening (290). Only in the light of such a recognition can Rennie free herself of their power and come to terms with her own male-identified tendency to reject other women because she sees her own weaknesses mirrored in theirs. Female bonding is not a concept that comes easily to Atwood's heroines, even in connection with their own mothers, as we have seen in previous chapters. But those who do discover such a source of strength are the true survivors in Atwood's fiction and poetry. Again, it requires the most dire circumstances to force Rennie to realise and then accept that her cellmate, Lora, is more noble in her acts of prostitution than is Rennie in her fastidious virtue. Lora is, in fact, a sister in the real sense, who pays for Rennie's survival with her body and, finally, perhaps with her life. It is surely a form of salvation or a redemption, a secular pietà, when Rennie huddles in a corner of her cell, holding the battered Lora in her arms, licking the encrusted blood away from the ruined face with her own tongue. Here Rennie reverses her lifelong practice of the lesson learned in childhood; she finally *touches* and doesn't look. The images are of giving birth as Rennie strains and pants, trying to push Lora back into life, but the actual birth is Rennie's own. Only in this unspoken declaration of sisterhood does Rennie fully assume her own humanity through a recognition of the humanity of others.

The ending of this novel is another example of Atwood's by now characteristic ambiguity. It is altogether possible that Rennie does not escape the prison, that she dies there, that the last paragraphs describing her return flight to Canada are merely the fancies of desperation. Jerome H. Rosenberg is quite possibly correct in his critical biography of Atwood when he maintains that the novel's conclusion represents '. . . a linguistic wish-fulfillment of Rennie's desires', an 'imagined future', a 'dream interlude', and that Rennie 'sits in her dark prison cell, rotting away to the bitter end'.[2] 'This is how I got here', the novel begins, and the 'here' is perhaps the cell as well as the metaphysical state of Rennie's regeneration. The flight home, then, is related in future tense, and Rennie's reflections include the enigmatic statement, 'She will never be rescued. She has already been rescued' (301). On the other hand, Rennie may be released. As Judith McCombs suggests in her article, 'Atwood's Fictive Portraits of the Artist', it is entirely possible that Rennie returns to Toronto in order to write *Bodily Harm*.[3] Atwood's point, we must conclude however, is that Rennie's death, whether immediate in the prison or imminent from cancer, is irrelevant. It is her vision which counts, and the confrontation with death is the existential affirmation that 'Zero is waiting somewhere, whoever said there was life everlasting; so why feel grateful? She doesn't have much time left, for anything. But neither does anyone else. She's paying attention, that's all' (301).

To 'pay attention', to look beneath surfaces, to touch and to tell are also imperatives for Offred of *The Handmaid's Tale*. Not paying attention, in fact, is the great fault of Offred's entire society, and the price exacted is the loss of freedom. By remaining uninvolved, by maintaining innocence, the people of a nation have forfeited human rights and become slaves in the near-future society of Gilead, an Orwellian dystopia dominated by the horrors of theocracy and puritanism. Big Brother, in this novel, is not simply an embodiment of patriarchy, nor of God, but rather of ideology in general; Gilead has permitted itself to be poisoned with radioactivity and with a far more pernicious entity: fanaticism that is political, religious and moral.

Atwood dedicates her novel to Perry Miller, whose books on the Puritans have informed American history, and to her own ancestor, Mary Webster, hanged for a witch in Connecticut. An atavistic puritanism, then, is the force which controls Gilead in the form of a profoundly immoral majority gone beserk. As in Orwell's *1984*, eroticism is prohibited on pain of death; pleasure is a crime against society; sex is valuable for the sole purpose of procreation in a depopulated world; books are burned; abortion and birth control are dim memories of some pagan past. Ugliness is universal; even nature itself has been tamed and ordered. Offred would like to tell us about the flowers, she says at one point in apology for the grim nature of her story, but even the tulips grow in fanatically-controlled rows like soldiers, their petals dropping 'one by one, like teeth' (161). People are compensated for the loss of nature and of sex, not exactly by 'two-minute Hates' in the Ministry of Truth as in Orwell's novel, but by analogous 'Prayvaganzas' and 'Salvaging' ceremonies in which the congregation participates in the ritual murder by dismemberment of arbitrarily-selected scapegoats, much like the victims in nightmare visions from Euripides' *Bacchae* to Shirley Jackson's 'The Lottery'. Thus, collusion is insured; the individual is truly a part of the whole and shares responsibility for every aspect of the system, including the perpetration of atrocity.

The real collusion, however, is in avoidance of responsibility. What was true for Rennie and for Annette of 'A Travel Piece' and for every other of Atwood's heroines in their insistence on their own non-involvement is here true for an entire society: 'There were marches, of course, a lot of women and some men. But they were smaller than you might have thought'. And Offred too is guilty, not of apathy, but of moral cowardice: 'I didn't go on any of the marches. . . . I had to think about them, my family, him and her. I did think about my family. I started doing more housework, more baking . . .' (189). Offred and other women have waited too long, have protested too little. They are reflections of Atwood's basic concern that victimisation, in a real sense, is at least partly a matter of choice. As Atwood writes in *Two-Headed Poems*, 'As for the women, who did not/want to be involved, they are involved./ It's that blood on the snow/which turns out to be not/some bludgeoned or machine-gunned/animal's, but your own/that does it' (83).

There is one heroic woman in *The Handmaid's Tale*, an equivalent to Lora in *Bodily Harm*, who does rebel; Moira protests repeatedly, escapes periodically, is tortured, but presumably survives. She represents an ideal for Offred, but also a source of guilt, for she accomplishes what Offred is too frightened to attempt. 'I'd like her to end with something daring and spectacular', says Offred, 'some outrage, something that would befit her. But as far as I know that didn't happen. I don't know how she ended, or even if she did, because I never saw her again' (262). Revolution or rebellion is precluded in Gilead, as in the real world, not only by terrorist tactics, but also by the suppression of news and the prevention of communication, on a personal level as well as a national one. In 'Notes Towards A Poem That Can Never Be Written', Atwood tells of 'the woman/they did not kill./Instead they sewed her face/shut, closed her mouth/to a hole the size of a straw,/and put her back on the streets,/a mute symbol' (*True Stories*, 50). Such, then, are the ultimate implications for Atwood's Little Mermaid of earlier poems and novels. The sacrifice of one's tongue, one's language, whether for love or for survival, is a price beyond reason.

So Offred is isolated and rendered mute by a prohibition against communication, and by her own solipsistic wish for survival. She finds it unthinkable to share experience with the commander's wives, who are all, like Serena Joy, incarnations of the Phyllis Schlaflys and Maribel Morgans of our own society, totally brain-washed yet unhappily aware of their imprisonment within their self-created ideological system. Offred makes some furtive attempts at communication with other Handmaids, but fear of betrayal prevents any meaningful exchange. As is the case with all of Atwood's previous heroines, Offred values her own physical survival above sisterhood, and in so doing sacrifices her own integrity, that which is, for Atwood, more crucial even than life.

The price for non-involvement in fact is slavery, and Offred, along with almost all other women in Gilead, has forfeited, not only freedom, but her identity and even parts of her memory as well. Women, in particular, seem to have forgotten that they ever had roles other than those determined for them by some vaguely-defined hierarchy of government. They have lost their very names; the Handmaids, in particular, are known by patronymics composed of the possessive preposition and a man's first name. All civil rights, including even the ownership of the most insignificant personal property, are cancelled. All the women wear uniforms, colour-coded to their functions: the 'Aunts' who run the 'Rachel and Leah Re-education Center', where the indoctrination of the Handmaids begins, wear brown. The 'Marthas' or house-keepers wear green; wives of officials or 'commanders' wear a kind of Virgin-Mary blue, perhaps an ironic reference to their infertility.

The Handmaids are identically dressed in red gowns which incongruously resemble religious habits; their faces are obscured by peaked hats which also function to prevent their seeing anything but what lies immediately in front of them. They are, in fact, personifications of a religious sacrifice, temple prostitutes doomed to a kind of purdah in perpetuity. As Atwood cautions in her poem, 'The Red Shirt', the colour red is highly significant: 'Young girls should not wear red./In some countries it is the color/of death; in others passion,/in others war, in others anger,/in others the sacrifice/of shed blood . . ./Dancing in red shoes will kill you' (*Two-Headed Poems*, 101). Offred's friend, Moira, perhaps the only woman in Gilead who retains her actual name, is surely intended to recall Moira Shearer who dances herself to death in 'The Red Shoes,' a film to which Atwood refers with great frequency, particularly in *Lady Oracle* and in *Second Words*. Handmaids turned malefactor in Gilead are hanged and suspended from a wall: 'Beneath the hems of the dresses the feet dangle, two pairs of red shoes. . . . If it weren't for the ropes and the sacks it could be a kind of dance, a ballet. . . . They look like showbiz' (289). 'I don't want to be a dancer', Offred later declares (298).

Perhaps the greatest deprivation of personal property, given Atwood's system of symbolism in all her novels and in her poetry, is that of the mirror, that instrument for establishing identity, for seeing into the truth about one's self. In *Bodily Harm*, Rennie and Lora have no mirror in their prison cell, and this requires that they depend upon each other for reflection. They literally must see themselves through each other's eyes in order to reassure themselves that they exist. Offred has no such partner, and her only vision of herself is fleetingly captured in reflective surfaces of windows surreptitiously regarded in passing. She is like the speaker in Atwood's poem, 'Marrying the Hangman', who observes that 'To live in prison is to live without mirrors. To live/without mirrors is to live without the self . . .' (*Two-Headed Poems*, 49).

But despite her isolation, despite her lack of a reflection either in a mirror or in the eyes of a friend, Offred does not entirely 'live without a self'. She is able to somehow objectify her situation, to see it phenomenologically, to separate herself from an unbearable reality, this time in a salutary way. Even under the most dehumanising of circumstances, Offred retains a kind of dignity. Her job as 'handmaid', as was the job of Rachel's handmaid in the Old Testament, is to offer her body as a vessel for procreation. In a grotesque threesome with her aging commander and his sterile wife, Offred is a sacrificial victim in a ritual of insemination that is at once pornographic and asexual. As she lies almost fully clothed in her red habit between the open thighs of the wife and receives the attentions of the husband, his only nudity an open zipper, Offred remains aloof, vaguely interested in the obscenity of repressed eroticism. Kissing is forbidden, Offred observes, and 'this makes it bearable. One detaches oneself. One describes' (106). Always, Offred's descriptions are a study in ironic understatement, her detached humour a foil to the horrific nature of events. 'Sanity is a valuable possession', she says, 'I hoard it the way people once hoarded money. I save it so I will have enough when the time comes' (119).

However, while Offred is clearly a victim, characteristic of Atwood's fiction is the message that victims in general are somehow implicated, at least partly responsible for their state. Man's inhumanity to man, and to women, does not absolve women from complicity. The control agency in this novel is, not the commanders, but 'the Aunts', who run their re-education centres with cattle prods, torture techniques, and brain washing slogans. The nursery-rhyme indoctrination for women, attributed by the Aunts to their hero, Saint Paul, is 'From each according to *her* ability; to each according to *his* need' (127). Surely Atwood intends her reader to recall the 'total woman' mentality, popularised in the early 60s to counteract an emerging feminism. Yet Atwood does not exonerate a radical feminist movement either, for it is this agent which instituted the original book burnings which have led to the universal censorship which characterises Gilead. Offred recalls her feminist mother's participation in a kind of witch's sabbath, a midnight ceremony of destruction in the name of anti-pornography. In the light of the burning books, 'the faces were happy, ecstatic almost. Fire can do that'. The child, before her name was Offred, is also allowed to add to the pyre: 'I threw the magazine into the flames. It riffled open in the wind of its burning; big flakes of paper came loose, sailed into the air, still on fire, parts of women's bodies, turning to black ash, in the air, before my eyes' (48–49). A 'women's culture', elements of which dominate in Gilead, can be as dangerous, Atwood indicates, as any other rigidly enforced system based on ideology. The 'Salvaging', for Atwood, is no more acceptable because a man is torn to bits by women than if the reverse had been the case.

No one is exempt from guilt, no one is blameless, Atwood implies, when it comes to the creation of a Gilead. *The Handmaid's Tale* is a study of guilt and an anatomy of power, but it is also a novel about forgiveness, about 'who can do what to whom and be forgiven for it' (145). Offred's lover Nick redeems all men by his act of saving Offred, although it may mean his own death. He is a kind of Orpheus to her Eurydice, as he brings her out of the world of the dead. For this is also a novel about survival. Offred perhaps escapes, we learn from the novel's appendix which is set in a further and presumably better future in which women again participate as human beings in a basically benevolent society. Perhaps it is this element of forgiveness, the persistence of love even in a loveless world, which makes Atwood's later novels and poems so powerful. The political horror poems in *True Stories* are similarly balanced by poems that are tender beyond any of Atwood's earlier work. Atrocity itself, even death, are somehow cancelled by one's love for a child, a daughter, who names herself, 'your own name first,/your first naming, your first name,/your first word' (64). The word 'Love' is 'not enough but it will/have to do. It's a single/vowel in this metallic/silence, a mouth that says/O again and again in wonder/and pain, a breath, a finger-/grip on a cliffside' (*True Stories*, 83).

Like the protagonist of *Surfacing* or like Rennie in *Bodily Harm*, Offred surfaces, not at all perhaps in control of her world (her actual fate is as uncertain as that of Rennie; we do not learn whether she is recaptured or whether she makes her way through Canada to the freedom of Europe), but at least in control of herself, and certainly with the recognition that political confrontation is not merely a choice but a human responsibility. Her responsibility, as it was the responsibility for Rennie, and even for Orwell's Winston Smith before his destruction, is to report, to chronicle her time, to warn another world. Handmaids in Gilead are not permitted to read or write because, according to their catechism enforced by the Aunts, 'Pen is Envy'. To have in one's possession a pencil is to commit a crime against the state; to participate in a clandestine game of Scrabble is to chance disaster. But Offred knows by now that communication is imperative; she must assume a future audience: '. . . I keep on going with this sad and hungry and sordid, this limping and mutilated story, because after all I want you to hear it. . . . By telling you anything at all I'm at least believing in you. . . . Because I'm telling you this story I will your existence. I tell, therefore you are' (279). Offred finds an antiquated artifact, a tape recorder, and, over the music of Montavani, Elvis

Presley and Twisted Sister, she records her message: and I only am escaped alone to tell thee.

The very act of writing, of recording, is for Atwood as well as for her heroines, the final and irrevocable commitment to one's society and to one's own humanity. As Atwood has said, 'Far from thinking of writers as totally isolated individuals, I see them as inescapably connected with their society. The nature of the connection will vary – the writer may unconsciously reflect the society, he may consciously examine it and project ways of changing it; and the connection between the writer and society will increase in intensity as the society . . . becomes the "subject" of the writer'.[4] Society, surely, is Atwood's subject. Art, thus, in political, and cannot help but be. Language, in itself, is the ultimate affirmation and the greatest revolution. 'A word after a word/after a word is power' (*True Stories*, 64).

# 7 Atwood as Critic; Critics on Atwood

Given Atwood's literary philosophy concerning the morality of language and the political responsibility of the artist, which has been the focus of the foregoing chapters, the reader is right to expect that philosophy predominates in Atwood's critical books and essays as well. In spite of Atwood's disclaimers that she is not primarily a literary critic, that she prefers other kinds of writing, and that critical writing is 'too much like homework' (*Second Words*, 11), her achievements in this area are nevertheless significant. With the publication of *Survival: A Thematic Guide to Canadian Literature*, a volume she modestly describes as a guide for 'students and teachers in high schools, community colleges and universities' (11), Atwood helped to put Canada on the literary world map and contributed to an impetus for Canadian nationalism. As the author of other book reviews descriptive of the works of Canadian authors, many of which are collected in *Second Words*, Atwood contributed to an international recognition of the fact of a Canadian literary identity. With her reviews of books by women authors from Canada as well as from the United States, Atwood advanced the cause of a growing feminist literary tradition. Atwood as critic, then, is almost as influential as Atwood as poet and novelist.

Atwood writes in *Survival*, '. . . if a writer feels himself living in a place whose shape is unclear to him . . . one of his impulses will be to explore it, another will be to name it' (114). In *Survival*, Atwood explores and names her own 'ancestral totems', her own tradition and national identity through a study of Canadian literature. She discovers a tradition replete with images of victimisation: animals, Indians, women, Eskimos, settlers and explorers are all victims of one another or of nature, just as nature itself is a victim of human beings. As the pervasive symbol of American literature, according to Atwood, is the frontier, so the dominant image in Canadian fiction is survival, the unheroic survival of victimisation:

> . . . the main idea is the first one: hanging on,
> staying alive. Canadians are forever taking the
> national pulse like doctors at a sickbed: the aim is
> not to see whether the patient will live well but
> simply whether he will live at all. Our central idea is
> one which generates, not the excitement and sense
> of adventure or danger which The Frontier holds out
> . . . but an almost intolerable anxiety. Our stories
> are likely to be tales not of those who made it but of
> those who made it back, from the awful experience –
> the North, the snow-storm, the sinking ship – that
> killed everyone else. The survivor has no triumph or
> victory but the fact of this survival; he has little after
> his ordeal that he did not have before, except
> gratitude for having escaped with his life. (33)

The Canadian literary tradition is so victim oriented, Atwood states throughout *Survival*, largely because of Canada's political status as a colony. To be a 'colony', Atwood writes, is to be victimised, exploited, as 'an oppressed minority' (35). Atwood outlines what she terms 'Basic Victim Positions', from the denial of victimisation as Position One, through the process of recognition and confrontation, to the status of 'creative non-victim' of Position Four. The political significance of these victim positions is obvious, whether for Canadians or for any other 'oppressed minority', including women, as Atwood observes in her essay 'Mathews and Misrepresentation' (*Second Words*, 145). Atwood argues for Canadian nationalism through the analysis, not only of Canadian literature, but of how that literature reflects a Canadian psyche. (As always for Atwood, art is a mirror: 'The reader looks at the mirror and sees not the writer but himself; and behind his own image in the foreground, a reflection of the world he lives in' (15).)

Atwood's deeply political messages in *Survival* have met with a great deal of predictable criticism, from Canadians as well as others. The ramifications of the controversy over *Survival* are not a subject for this study, but they frequently centre on largely uninteresting quibbles over which authors ought to have been included, whether Atwood should have explored the works of more authors from the nineteenth and early twentieth centuries rather than those from the 1930s through to the end of the 60s[1] and whether or not she did or should have concentrated on authors published by House of Anansi to the exclusion of other Canadian writers.[2] Critics have also disagreed with her attempts to thematically classify what seems to them a more diverse literature than Atwood's classifications indicate. According to Frank Davey in *Margaret Atwood: A Feminist Poetics*, *Survival* is guilty of '. . . overly narrow cultural definitions' which present 'a unitary, Ontario-based centralist view of the literature. Atwood did not see Canada and its literature through the differing perspectives of its regions or the differing aesthetics of its writers, but attempted to explain Canada through a single theory based on a single symbolic image'.[3] Still others, including George Woodcock in his essay unfortunately titled 'Bashful But Bold: Notes on Margaret Atwood as Critic', take exception to the influence on Atwood of critic Northrop Frye and to what Woodcock interprets as an excessively polemical approach. *Survival*, writes Woodcock, 'is one of those mildly exasperating books in which a brilliant intelligence has been unable to put the brakes on its activity and has run far ahead of the task undertaken . . .'.[4] While giving Atwood much credit for her insights into Canadian literature, for her humour and wit, Woodcock nevertheless patronisingly concludes: 'Let us take her seriously, but not too seriously. . . . in her mutable way she has been a good and important [critic] at this crucial time in the development of our sense of a literary culture'.[5]

Atwood's own responses to the critical reactions of *Survival*, particularly those of Robin Mathews as published in *This Magazine*, are both dignified and angry. As she writes in 'Mathews and Misrepresentation', responding to such critics is 'like trying to get through a church stuffed with bread dough: sanctimonious perimeter, amorphous content' (*Second Words*, 129). To Mathews' charges of distortion, Atwood argues that she did not present the heroic and victorious aspects of Canadian literature because these simply do not exist within the canon; her intention, rather, is to represent the truth of what she sees:

> I feel that in order to change any society, you have to
> have a fairly general consciousness of what is wrong –
> or at least that *something* is wrong – among the
> members of the society; call it 'consciousness-raising'
> if you like; and an examination of the effects of the
> situation on the heads of those in the society. . . . In
> other words: to fight the Monster, you have to know
> that there is a Monster, and what it is like (both in
> its external and internalized manifestations). (*Second
> Words*, 147)

Most relevant for the purposes of this study is that in

*Survival* as in her other works, Atwood continues to 'fight the Monster'; like Perseus, she holds the reflective shield and asks us merely to look: 'Even the things we look at demand our participation, and our commitment . . . what can result is a "jailbreak," an escape from our old habits of looking at things, and a "recreation," a new way of seeing, experiencing and imaging – or imagining – which we ourselves have helped to shape' (*Survival*, 246).

An analysis of *Survival* is important, not only for the insight it gives into Atwood's moral and political stands, but for the clues it also provides for an interpretation of Atwood's imagery and style in the novels and poems. As has been discussed in Chapter 1, many of the traditions and images Atwood describes in *Survival* also occur, with significant transformations, in her own works: the 'Great Canadian Baby', the 'Triple Goddess', the journey underground, the pervasive sense of victimisation, and, certainly, the survival theme itself. In *Survival*, as always in Atwood's works, is the plea for a release from literary stereotypes, from the terrible Triple Goddess, from the inhibiting effects of myth accepted without question. Paradoxically, however, Atwood also incorporates these myths and traditions into her own work, and both *Survival* and *Second Words* provide a kind of record of the ways in which Canadian and other traditions have influenced Atwood herself.

In Atwood's essay on H. Rider Haggard, 'Superwoman Drawn and Quartered: The Early Forms of *She*' (reprinted in *Second Words*), we see a reflection of Atwood's own interest in romantic literature and the kind of Gothic imagery she employs in many of her poems and novels. Atwood's treatment of these same Gothic and romantic images, however, is always ironic, as most obviously is the case in *Lady Oracle*, which is a parody of the Gothic tradition, an inversion of romantic mythology. Atwood's essay, 'What's so Funny? Notes on Canadian Humour', provides a commentary on her own anti-Gothic novel as well as on such writers as H. Rider Haggard: 'Parody habitually works in a double-edged way: by trivializing a specific work or style whose original has pretensions to profundity, it allows the audience an escape from the magical and mysterious in art' (*Second Words*, 181). All of Atwood's works are, in some sense, parodies, critical of any ideology or literary style which has 'pretensions to profundity'. But her concerns, as we know most particularly from *True Stories*, *Bodily Harm*, and *The Handmaid's Tale*, go deeper than mere parody can convey. The objects of rebuke in these novels and poems are far more pernicious and evil than pretentious profundity, and Atwood's humour takes on that quality of what she calls 'survival laughter, born from conditions so awful that you either have to laugh or stick your head in the oven' (*Second Words*, 176). Atwood herself is the 'satirist' she defines in 'Canadian Humour' as the artist who wishes 'to arouse moral indignation with a view to reform', who aims 'to expose, rebuke and correct' (*Second Words*, 183).

Atwood as a critic of other writers does not 'expose and rebuke', or, at least, she does so very gently. Those for whom she reserves praise are rewarded for the kinds of 'truth' for which Atwood herself also searches. Her reviews of works by poet Adrienne Rich, for example, seem almost an echo of what reviewers have said of Atwood. Rich, according to Atwood, pursues 'the quest for something beyond myths, for the truths about men and women, about the I and the You, the He and the She, and more generally . . . about the powerless and the powerful' (*Second Words*, 161). Atwood's comments on the poetic style of Erica Jong are also indications of what Atwood values in her own work: Jong's style, Atwood writes, is 'tricky. . . . But a good magician's best trick is to leave some doubt in the minds of the audience: perhaps the magic is real, perhaps the magic *power* is real' (*Second Words*, 174). Atwood is less comfortable with such works as *Flying* by Kate Millett, which Atwood sees as 'a somewhat confused object lesson in the integration of the political and the personal'. Millett's confessional style, that aspect of her writing which is most opposite to Atwood's style, is for Atwood a mixed virtue; while she grants the 'insights and revelations' of Millett's prose, she also comments that 'you may wonder whether you've been caught by the Ancient Mariner' (*Second Words*, 212).

Atwood is not primarily a critic of individual authors so much as she is a critic of systems, whether artistic or ideological. Her best essays in *Second Words* are those which expose social and intellectual injustices and attempt to prescribe remedies or alternative ways of seeing. For Atwood, there is no institution, no matter how sacred or how immediate to her own philosophical orientation, which is above reproach or which would not benefit from self-examination. One such institution is feminism and the kind of approach to art taken by many feminist critics. In 'On Being a Woman Writer: Parodoxes and Dilemmas', Atwood expresses concern about the development of what she terms 'one-dimensional' feminist criticism, 'a way of approaching literature produced by women that would award points according to conformity or non-conformity to an ideological position' (*Second Words*, 192). Feminist critics are as guilty as other critics, Atwood implies, in their insistence on art as gender-determined; what is necessary, Atwood writes, is the 'development of a vocabulary that can treat structures made of words as though they are exactly that, not biological entities possessed of sexual organs' (*Second Words*, 198). Atwood refuses the feminist literary stereotypes of women as she refuses the stereotyped female characters of any other tradition; we must search, she says, for a heroine who is 'not a natural force, whether good or evil', but a woman who 'makes decisions, performs actions, causes as well as endures events, and has perhaps even some ambition, some creative power. . . . Women, both as characters and as people, must be allowed their imperfections' (*Second Words*, 227).

As Atwood states at several points in *Second Words*, she refuses the term 'role model', whether as applied to herself or to her characters. As we have seen in the foregoing chapters, Atwood's protagonists are human beings, women with a small 'w'; they most frequently constitute negative examples rather than role models. Most importantly, they do not represent Atwood herself, nor do they speak for her except conversely. A great many critics, feminist critics as well as others, have confused Atwood's heroines with Atwood. They have read *Surfacing* as a hymn to the Great Mother rather than as the psychologically-oriented case study it actually is. They have seen Lesje in *Life Before Man* as the spokeswoman for what they consider Atwood's philosophy: the human race 'has it coming'. Joan Foster of *Lady Oracle* has been seen as an autobiographical representation of Atwood's own literary career. Particularly feminist critics have interpreted Atwood's portrayals of victims as paradigmatic of the female condition. In an insistence on seeing Atwood as a confessional writer and her works as autobiographical statements, critics have overlooked the irony implicit in Atwood's work and have, thereby, largely misinterpreted her messages.

According to Atwood, both men and women critics have taken exception to her portrayals of men, but certainly male critics seem particularly threatened by Atwood's characterisations. Frank Davey, for example, has subtitled his book on Atwood 'A Feminist Poetics', but yet objects to Atwood's 'female/male dichotomy . . . and the profound mistrust of men articulated in "Liking Men".'[6] Other male reviewers are more subtle (or less honest); Philip Stratford in 'The Uses of Ambiguity', for example, merely refers to 'a rankling sense of alienation' which 'permeates all her fiction' and is 'expressed in the neurotic edginess of her prose'.[7] Similarly, John Wilson Foster criticises Atwood's poetry as 'barely controlled hysteria' which takes 'specifically feminine forms' and represents 'certain fashionable minority psychologies'.[8] Jerome Rosenberg in *Margaret Atwood* also wishes at times for some quality in Atwood's work that could only be interpreted as an idea of femininity: of *The Journals of Susanna Moodie*, he writes that the poems are completely devoid of 'love and compassion, of simple and realistic human warmth'. Rosenberg seeks an 'emotionally compelling language of faith' instead of the 'abstract, formalized language of reason'.[9] Too, Rosenberg and other male critics are particularly loath to see Atwood in terms of a female literary tradition, comparing her work to a tradition of male writers from William Blake to John Barth, rather than to authors which Atwood herself has credited as influential, including poets Margaret Avison, Adrienne Rich and Anne Sexton.

Atwood has made her own opinions clear on the subject of earlier male critics, particularly those who find curly hair, 'petite' stature and marital status of supreme literary importance. In an interview with Karla Hammond, Atwood says,

> I've been reviewed in the most viciously sexist ways – more so in Canada than in the States because American reviewers are suaver about the way they attack people. I've been called a Medusa, an Octopus, etc., the attack being: here is a woman who doesn't use words in a soft, compliant way; therefore, she is an evil witch. And I'm tired of it; but it's impossible to educate them. You're getting someone who really has a tremendous fear of women.[10]

Atwood takes this image of the woman writer as witch and turns it to her own advantage. In her essay, 'Witches', she celebrates the identification with her ancestor, Mary Webster, who was hanged for a witch but survived: 'She is my favorite ancestor, more dear to my heart even than the privateers and the massacred French Protestants, and if there's one thing I hope I've inherited from her, it's her neck' (*Second Words*, 331). All women writers, according to Atwood, are on trial for witchcraft:

> We still think of a powerful woman as an anomaly, a potentially dangerous anomaly; there is something subversive about such women, even when they take care to be good role models. They cannot have come by their power naturally, it is felt. They must have *got it from somewhere*. Women writers are particularly subject to such projections, for writing itself is uncanny: it uses words for evocation rather than for denotation; it is spell-making. A man who is good at it is a craftsman. A woman who is good at it is a dubious proposition. (*Second Words*, 331)

Atwood's essay on 'Witches' provides a crucial image for an understanding of her later novels and poems in particular. *The Handmaid's Tale* is dedicated to Mary Webster and its principal subject is the suppression of language, especially language as used by women. Women who think or speak, other than by rote, or who dare to write, are hanged in Gilead, just as they are tortured or killed in those countries which Atwood describes in *True Stories*. In 'Spelling', the poet teaches her daughter 'how to spell,/spelling,/how to make spells'. To what fate, she wonders, does she thereby condemn her daughter, and she thinks of 'Ancestress: the burning witch,/her mouth covered by leather/to strangle words' (*True Stories*, 63–64). Again, in 'Torture', we find the image of the silenced woman: the woman with her face sewn shut, and her mouth closed 'to a hole the size of a straw' (*True Stories*, 50). Similarly, in 'Notes Towards a Poem that Can Never be Written', Atwood describes the tortured and mutilated woman who is '. . . dying because she said./She is dying for the sake of the word./It is her body, silent/and fingerless, writing this poem' (*True Stories*, 67).

Atwood does not write pleasant 'feminine' poems; neither is she tolerant of that masculine collective, 'They', as I have noted in Chapter 1. Atwood's most frequent weapon against her critics, particularly those who accuse her of being 'mean to men', however, is humour. Women authors in general, including Atwood herself, she indicates, are on the whole kinder to men in fiction than male authors are to men. In her essay, 'Writing the Male Character', Atwood catalogues the 'heroes' of past literature, including *Hamlet*, *Macbeth* and *Faust*. 'How about the behaviour of the men in *Moll Flanders*', she asks; 'Is *A Sentimental Journey* about the quintessential wimp?' (*Second Words*, 421). Although Atwood states that her intention is to depict men fairly and realistically, that women should 'take the concerns of men as seriously as they expect men to take theirs, both as novelists and as inhabitants of this earth' (*Second Words*, 428), she also concludes that the critics are insatiable, that they demand an unrealistic portrayal of male characters: 'Captain Marvel without the Billy Batson *alter ego*; nothing less will do' (*Second Words*, 420).

Atwood's other sin as defined by numerous critics is a general pessimism, a negative outlook on the world. Atwood, however, considers herself a realist rather than a pessimist: 'What you think is pessimistic depends very largely on what you think is out there in the world' (*Second Words*, 349). In 'Witches', she promises a year's free subscription to the Amnesty International Bulletin to the next critic who accuses her of pessimism. The world as Atwood sees it is in fact a dangerous and hostile place, and the writer's job is to define and judge that world, not to see it through rose-coloured glasses. In an early review of Margaret Avison's poetry, Atwood justifies Avison's 'realism': the subject of poetry ought not to be '. . . a chocolate-covered poetic pill, guaranteed to taste nice, go down easily, and eliminate all need for effort' (*Second Words*, 22). What the critics, booksellers, and the 'media bunnies' would like, Atwood says in 'An End to Audience?', is an 'entertainment package', money-making and film-producing fiction written, not by authors with political views, but by 'elements', ciphers who lend their words to slogans on T-shirts, who provide 'writing to suck your thumb by' (*Second Words*, 355). Atwood prefers truth to lies and realism to romance; her intention is not to communicate pessimism, but to inform and instruct and, finally, to provide hope: 'Writing, no matter what its subject, is an act of faith . . . it's also an act of hope, the hope that things can be better than they are' (*Second Words*, 349). Words themselves, Atwood reiterates throughout *Murder in the Dark*, constitute the defeat of pessimism:

> Outside, the plague bulges, slops over, flows down the streets and so we stay here, holding on and holding on, to the one small thing which is not yet withering, not yet marked for death, this armful of words, *together*, *with*. This is as good as it gets, nothing can be better and so there's nothing to hope for, but I do it anyway. In the distance, beyond the war in the midground, there's a river, and some willows, in sunlight, and some hills. (*Murder in the Dark*, 57)

If the writer is, as Atwood contends, the moral agent, the judge, then suppression of that writer's words is the truly immoral act. Atwood faults religious groups which remove books from high school library shelves on the basis that they are sexually explicit or contain 'objectionable' language; it is the act of the censors which is, in fact, obscene. In *The Handmaid's Tale*, as in the actual and current situation, some feminist groups exercise the same faulty judgement, thereby forefeiting their own freedom along with that of both the writers and the reading audience. 'A country or a community which does not take serious literature seriously will lose it', Atwood writes (*Second Words*, 357). Atwood is surely thinking of the censors and the critics more than of the antagonistic lover in her poem 'Spell for the Director of Protocol': 'You would like to keep me/from saying anything: you would prefer it/if when I opened my mouth/nothing came out/but a white comic-strip balloon/with a question mark; or a blank button . . .' (*Procedures for Underground*, 45).

It now seems an understatement rather than a summary to repeat that Atwood is a political writer and a moral writer. Like a great many other serious modern poets, Wallace Stevens for example, Atwood creates a 'supreme fiction' which transcends religion. Art itself is 'the word', and the artist its vehicle, its priest:

> . . . art happens. It happens when you have the craft and the vocation. . . . It's the extra rabbit coming out of the hat, the one you didn't put there. It's Odysseus standing by the blood-filled trench, except that the blood is his own. It is bringing the dead to life and giving voices to those who lack them so that they may speak for themselves. It is not "expressing yourself." It is opening yourself, discarding your *self*, so that the language and the world may be evoked through you. . . . Writing is also a kind of sooth-saying, a truth-telling. It is a naming of the world, a reverse incarnation: the flesh becoming word. It's also a witnessing. *Come with me*, the writer

is saying to the reader. *There is a story I have to tell you, there is something you need to know.* (*Second Words*, 347–48)

Whether she is priest or witch – or both or neither – Atwood does have something terribly important to tell us, something we do, in fact, need to know.

# Notes

### Notes to Chapter 1

1.  Karla Hammond, 'An Interview with Margaret Atwood', *The American Poetry Review*, Vol. 8, No. 5 (September/October, 1979), p. 29.

2.  Ibid., p. 29.

3.  Joyce Carol Oates, 'Margaret Atwood: Poems and Poet', *New York Times Book Review*, 21 May 1978, pp. 15, 43–45.


### Notes to Chapter 2

1.  Nina Auerbach, *Romantic Imprisonment: Women and Other Glorified Outcasts* (New York, Columbia University Press, 1985), p. 133.

2.  Ibid., p. 138.

3.  Ibid., p. 140.

4.  Ibid., p. 164.

5.  Sherrill Grace, *Violent Duality: A Study of Margaret Atwood* (Montreal, Vehicule Press, 1980), p. 59.

6.  Robert Lecker, 'Janus Through the Looking Glass: Atwood's First Three Novels', *The Art of Margaret Atwood: Essays in Criticism*, eds Arnold E. Davidson and Cathy N. Davidson (Toronto, Anansi Press, 1981), pp. 179–80.

7.  Catherine McLay, 'The Dark Voyage: *The Edible Woman* as Romance', *The Art of Margaret Atwood: Essays in Criticism*, eds Arnold E. Davidson and Cathy N. Davidson (Toronto, Anansi Press, 1981), p. 138.

8.  Kim Chernin, *The Obsession: Reflections on the Tyranny of Slenderness* (New York, Harper & Row, 1981), p. 71.

9.  Linda Sandler, 'Interview with Margaret Atwood', *The Malahat Review*, 4 (January, 1977), p. 19.


### Notes to Chapter 3

1.  Graeme Gibson, *Eleven Canadian Novelists* (Toronto, Anansi Press, 1973), p. 29.

2.  Ibid., p. 22.

3. Annis Pratt, '*Surfacing* and the Rebirth Journey', *The Art of Margaret Atwood: Essays in Criticism*, eds Arnold E. Davidson and Cathy N. Davidson (Toronto, Anansi Press, 1981), p. 151.

4. Ibid., p. 157.

5. Annis Pratt, *Archetypal Patterns in Women's Fiction* (Bloomington, Indiana University Press, 1981), p. 158.

6. Carol P. Christ, *Diving Deep and Surfacing: Women Writers on Spiritual Quest* (Boston, Beacon Press, 1980), p. 46.

7. Marie-Françoise Guedon, '*Surfacing*: Amerindian Themes and Shamanism', *Margaret Atwood: Language, Text, and System*, eds Sherrill E. Grace and Lorraine Weir (Vancouver, University of British Columbia Press, 1983), p. 91.

8. Jerome H. Rosenberg, *Margaret Atwood* (Boston, G. K. Hall, 1984), p. 122.

9. Barbara Hill Rigney, *Madness and Sexual Politics in the Feminist Novel* (Madison, University of Wisconsin Press, 1978).

10. Sherrill E. Grace, 'Margaret Atwood and the Poetics of Duplicity', *The Art of Margaret Atwood: Essays in Criticism*, eds Arnold E. Davidson and Cathy N. Davidson (Toronto, Anansi Press, 1981), p. 57.

**Notes to Chapter 4**

1. Linda Sandler, 'Interview with Margaret Atwood' , *The Malahat Review*, Vol. 4 (January, 1977), p. 19.

2. Jerome H. Rosenberg, *Margaret Atwood* (Boston, G. K. Hall, 1984), p. 116.

3. Ibid., p. 112.

4. Judith McCombs, 'Atwood's Haunted Sequences: *The Circle Game*, *The Journals of Susanna Moodie*', and *Power Politics*, *The Art of Margaret Atwood: Essays in Criticism*, eds Arnold E. Davidson and Cathy N. Davidson (Toronto, Anansi Press, 1981), pp. 36–37.

5. Clara Thomas, '*Lady Oracle*: The Narrative of a Fool-Heroine', *The Art of Margaret Atwood: Essays in Criticism*, eds Arnold E. Davidson and Cathy N. Davidson (Toronto, Anansi Press, 1981), p. 173.

6. Robert Lecker, 'Janus Through the Looking Glass: Atwood's First Three Novels', *The Art of Margaret Atwood: Essays in Criticism*, eds Arnold E. Davidson and Cathy N. Davidson (Toronto, Anansi Press, 1981), p. 203.

**Notes to Chapter 5**

1. Linda Hutcheon, 'From Poetic to Narrative Structures: The Novels of Margaret Atwood', *Margaret Atwood: Language, Text, and System*, eds

Sherrill E. Grace and Lorraine Weir (Vancouver, University of British Columbia Press, 1983), p. 29.

2. Frank Davey, *Margaret Atwood: A Feminist Poetics* (Vancouver, Talonbooks, 1984), p. 92.

3. Sherrill Grace, *Violent Duality: A Study of Margaret Atwood* (Montreal, Vehicule Press, 1980), p. 135.


## Notes to Chapter 6

1. Sherrill Grace, *Violent Duality: A Study of Margaret Atwood* (Montreal, Vehicule Press, 1980), p. 67.

2. Jerome H. Rosenberg, *Margaret Atwood* (Boston, G. K. Hall, 1984), p. 92.

3. Judith McCombs, 'Atwood's Fictive Portraits of the Artist: From Victim to Surfacer, From Oracle to Birth', *Women's Studies*, Vol. 12 (1986), pp. 69–88.

4. Margaret Atwood, 'Surviving the Critics', *This Magazine is About Schools* (1973), p. 33.


## Notes to Chapter 7

1. Sherrill Grace, *Violent Duality: A Study of Margaret Atwood* (Montreal, Vehicule Press, 1980), p. 1.

2. Frank Davey, *Margaret Atwood: A Feminist Poetics* (Vancouver, Talonbooks, 1984), p. 153.

3. Ibid., p. 154.

4. George Woodcock, 'Bashful but Bold: Notes on Margaret Atwood as Literary Critics', *The Art of Margaret Atwood: Essays in Criticism*, eds Arnold E. Davidson and Cathy N. Davidson (Toronto, Anansi, 1981), p. 237.

5. Ibid., p. 241.

6. Frank Davey, op. cit., p. 163.

7. Philip Stratford, 'The uses of Ambiguity: Margaret Atwood and Hubert Aquin' *Margaret Atwood: Language, Text, and System*, eds Sherrill E. Grace and Lorraine Weir (Vancouver, University of British Columbia Press, 1983), p. 113.

8. John Wilson Foster, 'The Poetry of Margaret Atwood', *Canadian Literature*, Vol. 74 (1977), p. 5.

9. Jerome H. Rosenberg, *Margaret Atwood* (Boston, G. K. Hall, 1984), p. 50.

10. Karla Hammond, 'An Interview with Margaret Atwood', *The American Poetry Review*, Vol. 8, No. 5 (September/October, 1979), p. 29.

# Bibliography

## Primary Works

(All references are to the following editions. Paperback books were used when possible.)

### Poetry

*Double-Persephone* (Toronto, Hawkshead Press, 1961).
*Murder in the Dark: Short Fictions and Prose Poems* (Toronto, Coach House Press, 1983).
*Power Politics* (New York, Harper and Row, 1973).
*Procedures for Underground* (Boston, Little, Brown and Company, 1970).
*Selected Poems* (New York, Simon and Schuster, 1978).
*The Animals in That Country* (Boston, Little, Brown and Company, 1968).
*The Circle Game* (Toronto, Anansi, 1978).
*The Journals of Susanna Moodie* (Toronto, Oxford University Press, 1970).
*True Stories* (New York, Simon and Schuster, 1981).
*Two-Headed Poems* (New York, Simon and Schuster, 1978).
*You Are Happy* (New York, Harper and Row, 1974).

### Novels and Short Stories

*Bluebeard's Egg* (Toronto, McClelland and Stewart, 1983).
*Bodily Harm* (New York, Bantam, 1983).
*Dancing Girls and Other Stories* (New York, Bantam, 1985).
*Lady Oracle* (New York, Avon, 1978).
*Life Before Man* (New York, Warner, 1983).
*Surfacing* (New York, Popular Library, 1976).
*The Edible Woman* (New York, Popular Library, 1976).
*The Handmaid's Tale* (Toronto, McClelland and Stewart, 1985).

**Non-fiction**

*Second Words* (Toronto, Anansi, 1983).
*Survival: A Thematic Guide to Canadian Literature* (Toronto, Anansi, 1972).

## Secondary Sources

Auerbach, Nina, *Romantic Imprisonment: Women and Other Glorified Outcasts* (New York, Columbia University Press, 1985).

Chernin, Kim, *The Obsession: Reflections on the Tyranny of Slenderness* (New York, Harper and Row, 1981).

Christ, Carol, *Diving Deep and Surfacing: Women Writers on Spiritual Quest* (Boston, Beacon Press, 1980).

——, 'Margaret Atwood: The Surfacing of Women's Spiritual Quest and Vision', *Signs* 2 (Winter, 1976), pp. 316–30.

Davey, Frank, *Margaret Atwood: A Feminist Poetics* (Vancouver, Talonbooks, 1984).

Davidson, Arnold E. and Davidson, Cathy N. (eds), *The Art of Margaret Atwood: Essays in Criticism* (Toronto, Anansi, 1981).

Foster, John Wilson, 'The Poetry of Margaret Atwood', *Canadian Literature*, 74 (Autumn, 1977), pp. 5–20.

Gibson, Graeme, *Eleven Canadian Novelists* (Toronto, Anansi, 1973).

Grace, Sherrill E., *Violent Duality: A Study of Margaret Atwood* (Montreal, Vehicule Press, 1980).

Grace, Sherrill E. and Lorraine Weir (eds), *Margaret Atwood: Language, Text, and System* (Vancouver, University of British Columbua Press, 1983).

Hammond, Karla, 'An Interview with Margaret Atwood', *American Poetry Review*, 8 (September/October, 1979), pp. 27–29.

Horne, Alan J., 'Margaret Atwood: An Annotated Bibliography', *The Annotated Bibliography of Canada's Major Authors*, eds Robert Lecker and Jack David (Downsview, Ontario, ECW Press, 1979 and 1980), Vols 1 and 2.

Juhasz, Suzanne, 'Renunciation Transformed, the Dickinson Heritage: Emily Dickinson and Margaret Atwood', *Women's Studies*, 12 (1986), pp. 251–70.

Mandel, Eli, 'Atwood Gothic', *The Malahat Review*, 41 (January, 1977), pp. 165–74.

Mathews, Robin, 'Survival and Struggle in Canadian Literature', *This Magazine is About Schools*, 6 (Winter, 1972–73), pp. 109–24.

McCombs, Judith, 'Atwood's Fictive Portraits of the Artist: From Victim to Surfacer, from Oracle to Birth', *Women's Studies*, 12 (1986), pp. 69–88.

Oates, Joyce Carol, 'Margaret Atwood: Poems and Poet', *New York Times Book Review*, 21 (May 1978), pp. 15, 43–45.

Pratt, Annis, *Archetypal Patterns in Women's Fiction* (Bloomington, Indiana University Press, 1981).

Rigney, Barbara Hill, *Lilith's Daughters: Women and Religion in Contemporary Fiction* (Madison, University of Wisconsin Press, 1982).

——, *Madness and Sexual Politics in the Feminist Novel: Studies in Brontë, Woolf, Lessing and Atwood* (Madison, University of Wisconsin Press, 1978).

Rosenberg, Jerome H., *Margaret Atwood* (Boston, G. K. Hall, 1984).

Rubenstein, Roberta, '*Surfacing*: Margaret Atwood's Journey to the Interior', *Modern Fiction Studies* 22 (Autumn, 1976), pp. 387–99.

Sandler, Linda, 'Interview with Margaret Atwood', *Malahat Review* 41 (January, 1977), pp. 7–27.

# Index